Decentralized Finance

Fundamentals, Ecosystems, and Innovations

Decentralized Finance

Fundamentals, Ecosystems, and Innovations

All Rights Reserved

Copyright © 2024 Engin Demirel, Ph.D.

All rights reserved. No part of this book may be reproduced, transmitted, or stored in any form or by any means, whether graphic, electronic, or mechanical, including photocopying, recording, or through any information storage and retrieval system, without the prior express written consent of the publisher, except for brief quotations used in critical articles or reviews.

Table of Contents

Table of Contents 3
List of Tables 10
List of Figures 10
Abstract 11
Introduction 12
Foundation of DeFi: Blockchain Technology 13
    Key Features of Blockchain Technology in DeFi 13
        Immutable Ledger 13
        Decentralization 14
    Key Factors Influencing Market Capitalization of DeFi: 14
    Key Factors Affecting Yield Returns: 16
        Supply and Demand Dynamics 17
        Platform-Specific Incentives 17
        Liquidity Pool Composition 17
        Impermanent Loss 17
        Platform Utilization Rate 18
        Smart Contract Risks 18
        Market Volatility 18
        Tokenomics and Governance 18
    Risks Associated with DeFi Yield Farming 19
        Smart Contract Risks 19
        Impermanent Loss 19
        Market Volatility 20
        Platform-Specific Risks 20
        Regulatory Risks 20
        Counterparty Risk 20
Core Components of DeFi 22
    Smart Contracts 22
    Roles of Smart Contracts in DeFi 23
        Automated Market Makers (AMMs) 23
            Key Concepts of AMMs 23
            How AMMs Work: A Step-by-Step Process 25
            Advantages of AMMs 26
            Challenges and Risks of AMMs 26
            Popular AMM Platforms 27
            Bancor 28
        Hacking and Fraud Incidents Related to AMM Platforms 35
            Technical Aspects 35
            Risk Management 35
            User Experience 36

Regulatory Landscape 36
Automated Market Makers (AMMs) Algorithms 36
    Constant Product Market Maker (CPMM) 37
    Constant Sum Market Maker (CSMM) 39
    Hybrid Functions (e.g., Curve's StableSwap) 40
    Constant Mean Market Maker 42
    Proactive Market Maker (PMM) 44
    Dynamic Automated Market Maker (DAMM) 45
    StableSwap Invariant (Advanced Implementations) 47
    Liquidity-Sensitive AMM (LS-AMM) 48
    Order Book Hybrid AMM 49
    Multi-Curve AMM 50
    Oracle-Based AMM 52
    Time-Weighted Average Price (TWAP) AMM 53
    Continuous Function Market Makers (CFMMs) 54
    Rebalancing AMM 55
    Structured AMM (SAMM) 56
    Stochastic AMM (S-AMM) 57
    Composable AMM (C-AMM) 59
    Elastic AMM (E-AMM) 60
    Pareto-Optimal AMM 61
    Machine Learning-Driven AMM 62
  Traditional market maker and an Automated Market Maker ... 65
    Traditional Financial Market Maker: 65
    Automated Market Maker (AMM): 66
    Pricing Mechanism 67
    Liquidity Provision 67
    Environment and Application 68
    Risks and Challenges 68
Machine Learning-Driven Automated Market Makers 69
  Key Concepts and Components of ML-AMMs 69
  Types of Machine Learning Models Used in ML-AMMs 70
  Advantages of Machine Learning Models 72
  Disadvantages and Challenges of ML-AMMs 72
  Use Cases for ML-AMMs 73
  Examples of Machine Learning-Driven Automated MM 74
  Training Machine Learning-Driven Automated MM 75
    Types of Data Needed: 76
    Data Sources: 76
    Model Selection 77
    Model Training 77
    Evaluation and Testing 80
    Deployment 81

- Deployment Steps: 81
- Continuous Learning and Improvement............................81
- Objectives for Machine Learning-Driven Automated MM 82
  - Price Prediction..82
  - Volatility Prediction 83
  - Risk Management 83
  - Liquidity Optimization 84
- Decentralized Exchanges (DEXs) 86
  - Key Characteristics of DEXs: 86
  - How Do DEXs Work? 86
    - Order Book-Based DEXs 87
    - Automated Market Maker (AMM)-Based DEXs...........88
    - Advantages of Decentralized Exchanges 89
    - Disadvantages of Decentralized Exchanges.................89
  - Examples of Decentralized Exchanges 90
    - Uniswap..90
    - SushiSwap 90
    - PancakeSwap..91
    - Curve Finance 91
    - Balancer..91
  - Comparing DEXs with Centralized Exchanges (CEXs).....................92
  - The Future of Decentralized Exchanges 93
    - Mechanisms for Achieving Cross-Chain Compatibility 94
    - Challenges in Cross-Chain Compatibility.....................95
    - Examples of Cross-Chain Projects in DeFi...................96
    - Layer 2 Solutions in DeFi DEXs 98
    - Types of Layer 2 Solutions for DeFi DEXs...................98
    - How Layer 2 Solutions Enhance DEX Performance 100
    - Examples of DEXs Using Layer 2 Solutions 101
    - Challenges and Considerations 101
  - Enhanced User Interfaces (UIs) in DeFi DEXs 103
    - Importance of Enhanced User Interfaces in DeFi DEXs 103
    - Key Features of Enhanced UIs in DeFi DEXs.............104
    - Examples of DEXs with Enhanced UIs 105
      - Uniswap Interface: 105
      - SushiSwap Interface 106
      - 1inch Exchange 106
      - Curve Finance Interface: 107
      - dYdX Interface:..107
    - Challenges in Enhancing UIs for DeFi DEXs.............107
      - Integration with Traditional Finance in DeFi DEXs: 110
      - Models for Integrating DeFi DEXs with Traditional Finance111
      - Challenges in DeFi-Traditional Finance Integration..............113

- DeFi DEXs and Traditional Finance Integration Examples ... 114
- Outlook for DeFi DEXs and Traditional Finance Integration 115
- Advanced Financial Instruments in DeFi DEXs ... 117
- Benefits of Advanced Financial Instruments in DeFi DEXs . 119
- Challenges of Advanced Instruments in DeFi DEXs ... 121
- Governance and Decentralization in DeFi DEXs ... 123
- Governance and Decentralization in DeFi DEXs ... 123
  - Common Governance Models in DeFi DEXs ... 125
  - Governance Processes and Features in DeFi DEXs ... 126
  - Examples of DeFi DEXs with Governance Models ... 128
  - Challenges in Governance and Decentralization ... 129
- Lending and Borrowing Platforms ... 132
  - Details of Lending and Borrowing Platforms ... 133
  - How Lending and Borrowing Platforms Work ... 134
  - Types of Lending and Borrowing Platforms ... 135
  - Benefits of DeFi Lending and Borrowing Platforms ... 136
  - Risks and Challenges ... 137
- Stablecoins ... 140
  - Definition and Basic Concepts ... 141
  - Types of Stablecoins ... 141
  - How Stablecoins Work ... 143
  - Fiat-Collateralized Stablecoins ... 144
    - Backing Mechanism of Fiat-Collateralized Stablecoins ... 145
  - Crypto-Collateralized Stablecoins ... 148
  - Algorithmic (Non-Collateralized) Stablecoins ... 152
  - Benefits of Stablecoins ... 156
  - Risks and Challenges ... 157
  - Key Stablecoins in the Market ... 158
  - Importance of Stablecoins in the Financial Ecosystem ... 159
  - The Future of Stablecoins ... 161
- Yield Farming ... 163
  - Details of yield farming ... 163
  - How Yield Farming Works: The Role of Liquidity Pools ... 164
  - Yield farming typically involves the following steps ... 164
  - Types of Yield Farming Strategies ... 166
  - Benefits of Yield Farming ... 167
  - Risks and Challenges ... 168
  - Popular Yield Farming Platforms ... 169
  - The Future of Yield Farming ... 170
- Governance Tokens ... 172
  - How Governance Tokens Work ... 173
  - Distribution of Governance Tokens ... 174
  - Benefits of Governance Tokens ... 175

- Risks and Challenges of Governance Tokens 176
- The Role of Governance Tokens in DeFi 178
- Future Developments in Governance Tokens 179
- Interoperability 181
  - Why is Interoperability Important? 181
  - How Interoperability Works 182
  - Key Projects and Protocols Promoting Interoperability 183
  - Benefits of Interoperability 185
  - Challenges and Risks of Interoperability 186
  - Future of Interoperability 187
  - New Trends in DeFi 187
- DeFi and Traditional İnvestment 189
  - DeFi and Fixed Income Securities 189
    - Risk Profile 189
    - Return on Investment 189
    - Liquidity 190
    - Complexity 190
    - Regulation and Security 190
  - DeFi and Stock Dividend Returns 191
    - Risk Profile 191
    - Return on Investment 191
    - Liquidity 192
    - Complexity 192
    - Regulatory and Legal Framework 192
  - DeFi and Real Asset Returns (Gold and Silver) 193
    - Risk Profile 193
    - Return on Investment 194
    - Liquidity 194
    - Complexity 194
    - Regulatory and Legal Framework 195
  - DeFi yield and Real Estate Returns 196
    - Risk Profile 196
    - Return on Investment 196
    - Liquidity 196
    - Complexity 197
    - Regulatory and Legal Framework 197
  - DeFi Platforms and Savings Accounts 198
    - Risk Profile 198
    - Return on Investment 198
    - Liquidity 198
    - Complexity 199
    - Regulatory and Legal Framework 199
  - Synthetic Assets and Decentralized Derivatives 200

- Risk Profile 200
- Return on Investment 200
- Complexity 201
- Liquidity 201
- Regulatory and Legal Framework 201
- DeFi Platforms and REITs 202
  - Market Risk 202
  - Liquidity Risk 203
  - Regulatory Risk 203
  - Complexity 203
  - Security Risks 204
  - Return on Investment 204
  - Diversification 205
  - Tax Considerations 205
- DeFi Yields and Certificates of Deposit (CDs) 207
  - Market Risk 207
  - Liquidity Risk 208
  - Regulatory Risk 208
  - Complexity 208
  - Security Risks 209
  - Return on Investment 209
  - Tax Considerations 209
  - Liquidity Considerations 210
- Popular Blockchains Used in DeFi 212
  - Ethereum 212
  - Binance Smart Chain (BSC) 212
  - Solana 212
  - Polkadot 213
  - Avalanche (AVAX) 213
  - Terra (LUNA) 214
  - Fantom (FTM) 214
  - Cardano (ADA) 215
  - Algorand (ALGO) 215
  - Tezos (XTZ) 216
  - Harmony (ONE) 216
  - Near Protocol (NEAR) 217
  - MultiversX 217
  - Celo (CELO) 218
  - Arbitrum 218
  - Optimism 219
  - Arweave (AR) 220
  - Internet Computer (ICP) 220
  - Ontology (ONT) 221

  Flow (FLOW) 221
  Kava (KAVA) 222
  ICON (ICX) 222
  Waves (WAVES) 223
  ThorChain (RUNE) 223
  EOS (EOS) 224
  Zilliqa (ZIL) 225
  Aptos (APT) 225
  Sui (SUI) 226
  Injective (INJ) 226
  Polygon zkEVM (MATIC) 227
Conclusion 229
References 230

List of Tables

Table 1: TVL, Token Utility, Security, and Innovation 15
Table 2: DeFi platforms Approximate Annualized Yield 15
Table 3: Comparative Analysis of Selected DeFi Platforms 32
Table 4: Platforms: Blockchain, Assets, Speeds, and Features 34
Table 5: Vulnerabilities in Major DeFi Platforms 35
Table 6: Automated MMA: Advantages, Disadvantages, Use Cases.....63
Table 7: Traditional Financial MM and Automated MM......................66
Table 8: Traditional Financial Market Maker vs Automated MM 69
Table 9: Machine Learning Applications for DeFi Platforms 74
Table 10: Comparison of DEXs and CEXs 92
Table 11: Stablecoin Types, Peg, Use Case and Issuer comparison.....158
Table 12: Comparative Analysis of Traditional Bonds vs. DeFi..........191
Table 13: Comparing the DeFi and dividend-paying stocks 193
Table 14: DeFi yield farming and investing in gold and silver 195
Table 15: DeFi yield farming and real estate investing 197
Table 16: DeFi platforms and savings accounts 199
Table 17: DeFi platforms and synthetic assets 202
Table 18: DeFi platforms and Real Estate Investment Trusts (REITs) 205
Table 19: DeFi platforms versus Certificates of Deposit (CDs)...........211
Table 20: Selected DeFi platform's features, advantages, drawbacks ..227

List of Figures

Figure 1: Types of Models in Machine Learning 81

Abstract

This book is an essential guide to understanding the Decentralized Finance (DeFi). As a revolutionary domain in financial technology, DeFi leverages blockchain to democratize access to financial services, breaking down traditional barriers and enabling more inclusive financial participation.

This book comprehensively covers the foundational aspects of blockchain technology that form the backbone of DeFi, as well as the intricate mechanisms behind decentralized exchanges, liquidity pools, and yield farming. It defines key terms, contrasts decentralized solutions with traditional financial systems, and examines how DeFi broadens the reach and capabilities of conventional financial markets. Topics such as stablecoins, governance tokens, and smart contracts are thoroughly explored to illuminate how these components work together to create innovative financial solutions. In addition to detailing the operational mechanics of DeFi platforms, the book provides a balanced discussion of their benefits and risks, making it an essential resource for anyone seeking to understand or engage with DeFi. Furthermore, the book delves into the future of DeFi, addressing the expansion of interoperability and the emergence of new protocols aimed at enhancing scalability and security.

Whether you are a finance professional, a student, or a curious investor, this book provides invaluable insights into a rapidly evolving field that promises to profoundly shape the financial sector.

I wrote this book in Amherst, Massachusetts, a town we truly loved. We created beautiful memories here, and we grew even fonder of this place thanks to the wonderful people we met. For this reason, I dedicate this book to the lovely town of Amherst and the University of Massachusetts.

Engin Demirel, Ph.D.
Amherst, MA, US

Introduction

DeFi, short for Decentralized Finance, refers to a broad category of financial services and applications that are built on blockchain technology, primarily using cryptocurrencies and smart contracts. Unlike traditional financial systems, which rely on central intermediaries like banks, DeFi aims to create an open, permissionless, and decentralized ecosystem where users can engage in financial activities without the need for intermediaries.

Key components and concepts within DeFi:

I. Smart Contracts: These are self-executing contracts with the terms of the agreement directly written into code. They automatically enforce and execute transactions when predefined conditions are met.

II. Decentralized Exchanges (DEXs): These are platforms that allow users to trade cryptocurrencies directly with each other without the need for a centralized authority or intermediary.

III. Lending and Borrowing Platforms: DeFi platforms allow users to lend their crypto assets to others in exchange for interest or borrow assets by providing collateral.

IV. Stablecoins: Cryptocurrencies that are pegged to a stable asset like the US dollar to minimize volatility, often used in DeFi applications for more predictable transactions.

V. Yield Farming: This involves providing liquidity to DeFi platforms in exchange for rewards, often in the form of additional tokens. It's a way for users to earn returns on their crypto holdings.

VI. Liquidity Pools: Pools of tokens locked in a smart contract that provide liquidity for decentralized trading, lending, or other activities.

VII. Governance Tokens: Many DeFi platforms issue tokens that give holders the right to vote on key decisions regarding the development and operation of the platform.

VIII. Interoperability: DeFi aims to create a more interconnected financial system where different platforms and applications can interact seamlessly through common standards and protocols.

Decentralized Finance, commonly known as DeFi, is a revolutionary financial system that leverages blockchain technology to recreate and enhance traditional financial systems in a decentralized and open manner.

Foundation of DeFi: Blockchain Technology

DeFi is built on blockchain technology, which is a distributed ledger that records all transactions across a network of computers. The most common blockchain used in DeFi is Ethereum, but other blockchains like Binance Smart Chain, Solana, and Polkadot are also popular.

- Immutable: Once data is recorded on the blockchain, it cannot be altered, ensuring transparency and trust.

- Decentralized: No single entity has control over the entire blockchain, making it resistant to censorship and manipulation.

Blockchain technology provides the essential features that enable DeFi to function in a decentralized, transparent, and secure manner. At its core, a blockchain is a distributed ledger or database that is maintained across a network of computers (nodes) rather than being controlled by a single entity. This decentralized nature of blockchains is what makes DeFi possible, allowing financial services to be executed without the need for traditional intermediaries like banks or brokers.

Key Features of Blockchain Technology in DeFi

Immutable Ledger

One of the most critical features of blockchain technology is its immutability. Once data is recorded on the blockchain, it cannot be altered, deleted, or tampered with. This is achieved through cryptographic techniques that secure the data and link each block of transactions to the previous one in a chain.

The immutability of the blockchain ensures that all transactions are permanently recorded and visible to anyone with access to the blockchain. This transparency fosters trust among users, as they can independently verify transactions and the integrity of the data without relying on a central authority.

The immutability also enhances security, as it prevents malicious actors from altering transaction records or attempting to commit fraud. Any attempt to change a transaction would require altering every subsequent block, which is computationally impractical and detectable by the network.

Decentralization

Decentralization is another foundational principle of blockchain technology, which means that control over the blockchain is distributed among all participants in the network, rather than being centralized in a single entity. This is achieved through a consensus mechanism, where all nodes in the network must agree on the validity of transactions before they are added to the blockchain.

- Censorship Resistance: Because no single entity controls the blockchain, it is resistant to censorship and government interference. This is particularly important in DeFi, where financial transactions can be conducted freely and without the risk of being blocked or reversed by a central authority.

- Reduction of Single Points of Failure: Decentralization reduces the risk associated with single points of failure, which are common in centralized systems. In a decentralized network, the failure or compromise of a single node does not jeopardize the entire network, ensuring continuous operation and reliability.

- Empowerment of Users: Decentralization empowers users by giving them direct control over their assets and transactions. In DeFi, users interact directly with smart contracts on the blockchain, removing the need for intermediaries and allowing for more inclusive and accessible financial services.

Key Factors Influencing Market Capitalization of DeFi:

Total Value Locked (TVL): The amount of assets locked "deposited" into a DeFi protocol.
Token Utility: The usefulness and demand for the platform's native token.
Adoption: The number of users and transactions on the platform.

Security: The platform's reputation for security and resilience against hacks.
Innovation: The platform's ability to introduce new features and products.
Market capitalization is just one factor to consider when evaluating DeFi platforms. It's essential to assess other factors such as fees, security, and the specific use cases of the platform. Table 1 shows comparison of selected DeFi Platforms: An Analysis of Total Value Locked (TVL), Token Utility, Security, and Innovation.

Table 1: TVL, Token Utility, Security, and Innovation

Platform	(TVL)	Token Utility	Security	Innovation
MakerDAO	High	Stablecoin (DAI) issuance, governance	Strong reputation	Continuous development of CDP system
Aave	High	Lending and borrowing, governance	Robust security measures	Introduction of new lending products and markets
Compound	High	Lending and borrowing, governance	Proven track record	Algorithmic, autonomous interest rate protocol
Uniswap	High	Decentralized exchange, governance	Community-driven security	Introduction of new features like flash swaps
Curve Finance	High	Stablecoin exchange, governance	focus on security	Development of new liquidity pools and strategies
Yearn Finance	High	Yield optimization, governance	Automated strategies	Continuous introduction of new vaults and strategies
Synthetix	Medium	Synthetic assets, governance	Focus on security and stability	Development of new synthetic assets and derivatives
SushiSwap	High	Decentralized exchange, governance	Community-driven security	Introduction of new features and partnerships
Pancake Swap	High	Exchange & governance	security measures	Constant updates a

Yield returns can fluctuate significantly due to market conditions, protocol changes, and other factors. The data provided below is based on historical performance and may not accurately reflect current yields. Table 2 shows annualized yield projections for major DeFi platforms.

Table 2: DeFi platforms Approximate Annualized Yield

Platform	Annualized Yield (USD) Dec. 2024
Aave	3-10%
Compound	2-8%
Yearn Finance	5-15% (varies across vaults)
MakerDAO	0.5-5%
Curve Finance	1-7%
Uniswap	1-5% (liquidity pools)
SushiSwap	2-10% (liquidity pools)
PancakeSwap	3-12% (liquidity pools)
Lido	4-8% (staking rewards)
Synthetix	3-10% (staking rewards)

Key Factors Affecting Yield Returns:

Yield returns on DeFi platforms can vary significantly based on several factors. Understanding these factors is crucial for investors looking to maximize their returns while managing the associated risks.

Interest Rates: The underlying interest rates on the platform's lending and borrowing markets.
Token Price Volatility: Fluctuations in the price of the platform's native token can impact overall returns.
Protocol Fees: Fees charged by the protocol can reduce potential yields.
Impermanent Loss: The risk of losing value due to price fluctuations in assets held in liquidity pools.
Risk Premium: Higher-risk platforms may offer higher yields to compensate for increased risk.

Key factors that influence yield returns in DeFi:

Supply and Demand Dynamics

The supply of and demand for assets or liquidity in a DeFi platform directly impacts the yield returns. High demand for borrowing an asset can lead to higher interest rates, thereby increasing yield returns for lenders or liquidity providers.

> Example: On a platform like Compound, if there is high demand for borrowing DAI (a stablecoin), the interest rate for lending DAI will rise, leading to higher returns for those providing DAI to the platform.

Platform-Specific Incentives

Many DeFi platforms offer additional incentives in the form of governance tokens or reward tokens to encourage participation. These rewards can significantly boost overall yield returns.

> Example: On platforms like Aave or Uniswap, liquidity providers may earn AAVE or UNI tokens, respectively, in addition to transaction fees or interest, enhancing the overall yield.

Liquidity Pool Composition

The composition and diversity of assets in a liquidity pool can impact the yields. Pools with more volatile assets may offer higher returns due to the increased risk, while pools with stable assets may offer lower, but more predictable, returns.

> Example: A liquidity pool with ETH and a stablecoin like USDC might offer lower returns compared to a pool with two volatile assets like DOGE and SHIB, reflecting the different risk profiles.

Impermanent Loss

Impermanent loss occurs when the value of assets in a liquidity pool diverges from the value they would have if held outside the pool. This can reduce the effective yield for liquidity providers, particularly in volatile markets.

> Example: If a liquidity provider deposits ETH and USDT into a pool and the price of ETH increases significantly, the provider might end up with less ETH when they withdraw, leading to a lower overall return.

Platform Utilization Rate

The utilization rate of a DeFi platform (the ratio of assets lent out to the total assets available) affects the interest rates and, consequently, the yields. A higher utilization rate typically leads to higher interest rates.

> Example: On a lending platform like Compound, if most of the DAI available for lending is borrowed, the interest rate for remaining DAI will increase, leading to higher yields for lenders.

Smart Contract Risks

The risk of bugs or vulnerabilities in the smart contracts that govern DeFi platforms can impact yield returns. If a platform is perceived as risky, yields may be higher to compensate for the additional risk.

> Example: A newly launched DeFi platform might offer higher yields to attract users, but these higher returns might come with the increased risk of potential smart contract failures.

Market Volatility

High market volatility can lead to fluctuations in yields, particularly for liquidity providers. Volatile markets may lead to more trading activity, increasing fees earned by liquidity providers, but also increasing the risk of impermanent loss.

> Example: During periods of high volatility, a platform like Uniswap may see increased trading volumes, leading to higher fees for liquidity providers, but also a higher chance of impermanent loss.

Tokenomics and Governance

The underlying "tokenomics" (refers to the study of how cryptocurrencies are structured and function within their ecosystems, encompassing aspects such as creation, distribution, supply, demand, and incentive mechanisms that influence their value and utility) and governance structure of a DeFi platform can influence yields. For example, if a platform's governance decides to reduce the issuance rate of reward tokens, this could reduce yields.

> Example: If a platform like Sushiswap decides to reduce the distribution of SUSHI tokens to liquidity providers, the overall yield might decrease, reflecting the lower rewards.

Risks Associated with DeFi Yield Farming

While DeFi platforms can offer attractive yields, they also come with significant risks. Here's a detailed look at the risks involved:

Smart Contract Risks

Smart contracts are the backbone of DeFi platforms, but they can be vulnerable to bugs, exploits. If a smart contract is compromised, users can lose their funds.

> Example: The 2020 hack of the bZx protocol (bZx is a decentralized finance (DeFi) protocol built on the Ethereum blockchain) resulted in the loss of millions of dollars due to a flaw in its smart contracts. In September 2020, bZx suffered an exploit where a bug in the iTokens (interest-bearing tokens within the bZx Protocol) duplication method was exploited. This situation marked the third hack that bZx experienced that year, each involving vulnerabilities in its smart contracts[1]

Impermanent Loss

Liquidity providers face the risk of impermanent loss when the prices of the assets in the liquidity pool change relative to each other. This can result in lower returns compared to simply holding the assets.

---

[1] https://nextrope.com/smart-contract-attacks-the-most-memorable-blockchain-hacks-of-all-time/

> Example: A liquidity provider in an ETH/USDC pool may experience impermanent loss if the price of ETH increases significantly relative to USDC, leading to a reduction in their ETH holdings when they withdraw.

Market Volatility

High market volatility can lead to sharp changes in the value of assets in DeFi platforms, affecting both the principal and the returns. This can be particularly risky for yield farmers who use leverage.

> Example: A sudden market crash could lead to a sharp drop in the value of assets being farmed, potentially wiping out gains or causing losses.

Platform-Specific Risks

Each DeFi platform has its own set of risks, including liquidity risks, governance risks, and the risk of regulatory changes. Users need to understand the specific risks associated with the platform they are using.

> Example: A platform with low liquidity might struggle to fulfill withdrawal requests, especially during times of high market stress, leading to delays or losses.

Regulatory Risks

The regulatory environment for DeFi is still evolving. Changes in regulations could impact the legality and operation of DeFi platforms, potentially leading to loss of funds or access.

> Example: A government crackdown on DeFi platforms could lead to platforms being shut down or restricted, affecting users' ability to access their funds. September 2023, the U.S. Commodity Futures Trading Commission (CFTC) charged three DeFi platforms "Opyn, Inc.", "ZeroEx, Inc.", and "Deridex, Inc." with operating unregistered platforms that allowed U.S. persons to trade digital asset derivatives[2].

---

[2] https://www.cftc.gov/PressRoom/PressReleases/8774-23

Counterparty Risk

While DeFi platforms are decentralized, they can still involve counterparty risks, especially in cases where centralized components are involved (e.g., oracles, custodial wallets).

Example: If an oracle that feeds price data to a DeFi platform is compromised, it could lead to incorrect valuations and potentially result in loss of funds for users. An attacker manipulated the price of stablecoins on Curve Finance's liquidity pools, which were used as price oracles by "Harvest Finance". This manipulation allowed the attacker to exploit Harvest Finance's vaults, resulting in a loss of approximately $33 million. Also, an attacker manipulated the price oracle of "Mango Markets", a decentralized exchange on the Solana blockchain, by inflating the value of the "MNGO" token. This allowed the attacker to borrow and withdraw approximately $117 million from the platform[3].

---

[3]https://www.chainalysis.com/blog/oracle-manipulation-attacks-rising

Core Components of DeFi

DeFi includes various applications and services, each serving a specific purpose within the decentralized financial ecosystem:

Smart Contracts

Smart contracts are self-executing contracts with the terms directly written into code. These contracts automatically enforce and execute transactions when certain conditions are met.

> Example: A smart contract could automatically release funds from a borrower's account to a lender when the loan repayment conditions are met.

Smart contracts are the backbone of DeFi, enabling the creation and operation of decentralized financial applications without the need for traditional intermediaries.

Key Features of Smart Contracts

- Automation: Smart contracts automatically execute predefined actions when certain conditions are met, eliminating the need for intermediaries or manual intervention.

- Transparency: The code of smart contracts is typically open source, allowing anyone to inspect and verify the rules and logic behind the contract.

- Immutability: Once deployed on a blockchain, smart contracts cannot be altered. This ensures that the contract's terms are consistent and cannot be tampered with by any party.

- Security: Smart contracts are secured by the underlying blockchain technology, which makes them resistant to censorship and fraud, although they are still vulnerable to bugs or manipulates.

Roles of Smart Contracts in DeFi

Smart contracts play various critical roles in enabling the functionality of DeFi platforms. Below are some of the key areas where smart contracts are used in DeFi:

Automated Market Makers (AMMs)

AMMs are decentralized exchanges (DEXs) that allow users to trade cryptocurrencies directly with a liquidity pool rather than relying on a traditional order book. Smart contracts in AMMs automatically manage the liquidity pool, determine prices, and execute trades based on a predefined algorithm.

Example: On platforms like "Uniswap" or "SushiSwap", smart contracts control the liquidity pools and use algorithms like the constant product formula to set the price of assets and facilitate trades between different tokens.

Key Concepts of AMMs
1. Liquidity Pools

At the core of AMMs are liquidity pools, which are collections of funds locked in a smart contract. These pools are used to facilitate trades on the AMM platform. A liquidity pool typically consists of two assets, which are used to create trading pairs (e.g., ETH/USDC).

Function: When users want to trade one asset for another, they interact with the liquidity pool instead of a traditional order book. The AMM uses a predefined mathematical formula to determine the price and facilitate the swap.

2. Liquidity Providers (LPs)

Liquidity providers are users who deposit equal values of two assets into a liquidity pool. In return, they receive liquidity provider (LP) tokens, representing their share in the pool. These LP tokens can be used to redeem their share of the pool at any time, along with a portion of the trading fees earned.

Incentives: LPs are incentivized by earning a portion of the transaction fees generated by trades that occur within the pool. Additionally, some platforms offer additional rewards in the form of governance tokens.

3. Pricing Mechanism

AMMs use algorithms to determine the price of assets within a pool. The most common pricing algorithm is the constant product formula, popularized by Uniswap.

Constant Product Formula ($x * y = k$): In this formula, x and y represent the quantities of the two assets in the pool, and k is a constant. The product of the quantities of the two assets must always equal k. When a trade is made, the quantities of the assets change, but the product (k) remains constant, which alters the price.

4. Slippage

Slippage refers to the difference between the expected price of a trade and the actual price executed. In AMMs, slippage occurs when large trades are executed in relatively low-liquidity pools, leading to significant price changes during the trade.

Management: Traders can set slippage tolerance levels, which cancel the trade if the slippage exceeds the acceptable range. High slippage can result in unfavorable prices for traders.

5. Impermanent Loss

Impermanent loss is a risk faced by liquidity providers when the price of the assets in the pool diverges from the price at which they were deposited. This loss is termed "impermanent" because it only becomes permanent if the liquidity provider withdraws their assets at this unfavorable price ratio.

Impact: If the price of one asset in the pool increases or decreases significantly, liquidity providers might end up with less value than they would have had by simply holding the assets outside the pool.

How AMMs Work: A Step-by-Step Process
Liquidity Provision:

A user decides to become a liquidity provider (LP) and deposits an equal value of two assets into a liquidity pool. For example, they might deposit $1,000 worth of ETH and $1,000 worth of USDC into an ETH/USDC pool.

In return, the LP receives "LP tokens" that represent their share of the pool. These tokens can be "redeemed" later for their share of the pool's assets and any accumulated fees.

Trading:

Another user wants to trade ETH for USDC. Instead of trading with another user, they interact directly with the liquidity pool.

The AMM algorithm calculates the exchange rate based on the current balance of ETH and USDC in the pool (using the constant product formula).

The trade is executed, increasing the pool's ETH balance and decreasing the USDC balance, which in turn changes the exchange rate slightly to reflect the new ratio of assets.

Fee Collection:

Each trade incurs a small fee (e.g., 0.3% on Uniswap), which is distributed proportionally to all LPs in the pool. This fee incentivizes liquidity provision.

Liquidity Provider Exit:

The LP can exit the pool at any time by redeeming their "LP tokens". They receive their share of the pool's assets, along with any fees earned during their time as an LP.

The value of the assets they receive may differ from what they initially deposited due to changes in the asset prices and impermanent loss.

Advantages of AMMs

Decentralization:

AMMs operate without the need for centralized intermediaries, allowing users to trade directly from their wallets. This reduces counterparty risk and promotes censorship resistance.

Continuous Liquidity:

Unlike traditional order books, which can suffer from low liquidity or thin order books, AMMs provide continuous liquidity as long as there are assets in the pool. This makes it easier for users to trade even in less popular markets.

Accessibility:

AMMs lower the barrier to entry for market making. Anyone with assets can provide liquidity and earn fees, democratizing the process and enabling broader participation in financial markets.

Simplicity:

The use of mathematical formulas like the constant product formula simplifies the trading process and eliminates the need for complex matching engines. Trades are executed automatically based on the liquidity in the pool.

Incentivization:

AMMs incentivize liquidity provision through fee sharing and, in some cases, additional rewards like governance tokens. This creates a self-sustaining ecosystem where liquidity providers are rewarded for their contributions.

Challenges and Risks of AMMs

Impermanent Loss:

As mentioned earlier, impermanent loss is a significant risk for liquidity providers. It occurs when the price of the assets in the pool changes relative to when they were deposited, potentially leading to a loss in value compared to simply holding the assets.

Slippage:

Large trades in low-liquidity pools can result in high slippage, where the price received by the trader differs significantly from the expected price. This can make AMMs less efficient for large trades compared to traditional exchanges.

Smart Contract Risks:

AMMs are powered by smart contracts, which can contain vulnerabilities or bugs. A flaw in the smart contract could be exploited by malicious actors, leading to loss of funds from the liquidity pool or users' wallets.

Price Manipulation:

AMMs can be susceptible to price manipulation, particularly through "flash loan attacks", where a large, temporary loan is used to manipulate the price within a liquidity pool. This can lead to significant losses for liquidity providers or traders.

Capital Inefficiency:

In some AMM models, a large amount of capital is required to maintain deep liquidity, especially for volatile assets. However, not all this capital is always fully utilized, leading to inefficiencies.

Popular AMM Platforms

Uniswap is one of the most well-known AMMs, using the constant product formula ($x * y = k$) to facilitate trades. It has become the backbone of decentralized trading on Ethereum, allowing users to trade any ERC-20 token pair.

SushiSwap is a fork of Uniswap that offers additional incentives to liquidity providers, including rewards in the form of SUSHI tokens. It also has added features like yield farming and staking.

Balancer4 allows users to create custom liquidity pools with up to eight different tokens, with varying weights. This flexibility makes it possible to design pools that better align with the user's investment strategy.

Also "Balancer" is a flexible AMM that allows users to create and manage liquidity pools with multiple tokens (up to eight) and adjustable weightings for each token. This enables a greater level of customization and efficiency compared to traditional AMMs that typically operate with 50/50 pools.

Curve Finance "Curve" is an AMM designed specifically for stablecoins, minimizing slippage and impermanent loss by using a formula optimized for assets that trade at similar prices. It is popular for swapping stablecoins like USDC, DAI, and USDT.

PancakeSwap is an AMM on the Binance Smart Chain (BSC), offering lower transaction fees and faster confirmations compared to Ethereum-based AMMs. It is one of the most popular DEXs on BSC.

Bancor5 is one of the first AMM platforms to be launched in the DeFi ecosystem. It introduced the concept of "smart tokens," which are tokens that can be converted automatically via smart contracts, without needing a counterparty. Bancor allows for single-sided liquidity provision, meaning users can provide liquidity with only one type of asset and still earn fees. Bancor offers protection against impermanent loss for liquidity providers. This feature is designed to compensate LPs for potential losses due to price fluctuations between the deposited assets. Unlike most AMMs, Bancor allows users to provide liquidity with just one token, simplifying the process and reducing the risks associated with providing liquidity in volatile pairs. Bancor's architecture supports cross-chain liquidity pools, allowing users to trade and provide liquidity across multiple blockchain networks.

Kyber Network6 is an on-chain liquidity protocol that aggregates liquidity from various sources to provide instant and secure token swaps

---

[4] https://balancer.fi
[5] https://bancor.network
[6] https://kyber.network

in DeFi applications. Unlike traditional AMMs, Kyber's protocol is designed to serve both users and liquidity providers by offering customizable liquidity pool options.

Kyber Dynamic Market Maker (DMM): This feature allows LPs to set their own fee tiers and adjust the dynamic fee based on market conditions, which can maximize returns during periods of high volatility and reduce impermanent loss. Liquidity Aggregation: Kyber aggregates liquidity from multiple sources, including professional market makers and reserves, ensuring competitive prices and deep liquidity. Integration with dApps: This Network is integrated into many decentralized applications, allowing users to trade tokens directly within those platforms.

Curve Finance is a specialized AMM designed for stablecoins and other assets that trade at similar prices. Its focus on minimizing slippage and impermanent loss makes it particularly popular for stablecoin swaps and for trading between assets like wrapped Bitcoin (wBTC) and Bitcoin derivatives.

Low Slippage: Curve's AMM model is optimized for assets that have low volatility relative to each other, resulting in lower slippage for large trades compared to other AMMs. Stablecoin Focus: Curve is the go-to platform for stablecoin trading, offering deep liquidity and low-cost swaps between popular stablecoins like USDT, USDC, DAI, and others. Integration with DeFi Ecosystem: Curve integrates with various DeFi protocols to enhance yield farming opportunities, often serving as a primary venue for stablecoin liquidity.

SushiSwap is a community-driven AMM that emerged as a fork of Uniswap. It differentiates itself by offering additional incentives for liquidity providers, including SUSHI token rewards, and by continuously expanding its suite of DeFi products.

SUSHI Rewards: In addition to earning fees, liquidity providers on SushiSwap receive SUSHI tokens as rewards, which can be staked to earn even more rewards in a process called "SushiBar." BentoBox: SushiSwap has introduced BentoBox, a vault for DeFi applications that allows for efficient capital utilization by enabling developers to build dApps on top of it, leveraging the liquidity within BentoBox. MISO (Minimal Initial Sushi Offering): MISO is SushiSwap's platform for launching new tokens, allowing projects to conduct fair and decentralized token sales.

PancakeSwap is the leading AMM and yield farming platform on the Binance Smart Chain (BSC). It offers a wide range of DeFi services, including token swaps, yield farming, lotteries, and non-fungible token (NFT) offerings. PancakeSwap is known for its lower transaction fees and faster confirmation times compared to Ethereum-based AMMs.

Low Fees and Fast Transactions: Being on BSC, PancakeSwap benefits from lower fees and faster transaction speeds, making it an attractive alternative to Ethereum-based platforms. Yield Farming and Syrup Pools: In addition to traditional liquidity provision, PancakeSwap offers yield farming opportunities through Syrup Pools, where users can stake CAKE tokens to earn rewards in various tokens. NFT Marketplace: PancakeSwap has an integrated NFT marketplace, allowing users to trade, buy, and sell NFTs directly on the platform.

Raydium[7] is a Solana-based AMM that integrates with Serum, a decentralized exchange (DEX) on Solana. Raydium offers high-speed and low-cost trading, leveraging Solana's high throughput and Serum's order book to provide a hybrid AMM/order book trading experience.

Raydium's integration with Serum allows it to tap into the order book of Serum DEX[8], combining the benefits of AMMs with the liquidity of a traditional order book exchange. Solana's blockchain is known for its high transaction throughput and low fees, making Raydium one of the fastest and most cost-effective AMMs. Also, Raydium offers yield farming opportunities, allowing users to stake RAY tokens or provide liquidity to earn rewards.

"1inch[9]" Liquidity Protocol is known as a DEX aggregator that finds the optimum prices across multiple decentralized exchanges, but it also

---

[7] https://raydium.io
[8] https://serum-dex.vercel.app
[9] https://1inch.io

offers its own AMM, the "1inch Liquidity Protocol". This protocol provides flexible pools with customizable fee structures and dynamic pricing models.

The 1inch platform aggregates liquidity from various DEXs to ensure that users get the best prices for their trades, reducing slippage and improving trade execution. Liquidity providers on 1inch can create and manage pools with customizable fees and pricing curves, allowing for more tailored liquidity provision strategies. 1inch's liquidity protocol is designed to minimize gas fees, making it more efficient and cost-effective for users, particularly on the Ethereum network.

QuickSwap is a layer-2 AMM built on the Polygon (formerly Matic) network, which offers fast and low-cost trading. QuickSwap operates similarly to Uniswap but benefits from the scalability and reduced transaction costs provided by Polygon.

QuickSwap leverages Polygon's layer-2 infrastructure to provide near-instant transactions with minimal fees, making it an attractive alternative for users looking to avoid Ethereum's high gas fees. QuickSwap supports a wide range of token pairs and offers yield farming opportunities, allowing users to earn "QUICK" tokens as rewards for providing liquidity. QuickSwap integrates with various cross-chain bridges (These structures are decentralized applications that enable the transfer of assets and data between distinct blockchain networks, facilitating interoperability within the blockchain ecosystem), allowing users to move assets between Ethereum, Polygon, and other supported networks seamlessly.

Table 3: Comparative Analysis of Selected DeFi Platforms

Platform	Key Features	Strengths	Weaknesses
Uniswap	Constant product formula	Pioneer, widely adopted	May have higher fees and slower transactions on Ethereum
SushiSwap	Additional incentives, yield farming	Community-driven, various DeFi services	May have similar challenges to Uniswap
Balancer	Flexible liquidity pools	Customization options	More complex to use for beginners
Curve Finance	Stablecoin focus, low slippage	Efficient for stablecoin swaps	Limited to stablecoins and similar assets
PancakeSwap	BSC-based, low fees	Fast transactions, various DeFi services	Limited to BSC
Bancor	Smart tokens, impermanent loss protection	Unique features	May have lower liquidity than larger platforms
Kyber Network	Liquidity aggregation	Competitive prices, integration with dApps	May have higher fees due to aggregation
Balancer	Multi-token pools, smart order routing	Customization options	More complex to use for beginners
Curve Finance	Stablecoin focus, low slippage	Efficient for stablecoin swaps	Limited to stablecoins and similar assets
SushiSwap	Additional incentives, yield farming	Community-driven, various DeFi services	May have similar challenges to Uniswap
PancakeSwap	BSC-based, low fees	Fast transactions, various DeFi services	Limited to BSC
DODO	PMM algorithm, single-sided liquidity	Better price stability, reduced slippage	May be less well-known than established platforms
Raydium	Solana-based, high-speed trading	Fast transactions, integration with Serum	Limited to Solana ecosystem
1inch Liquidity Protocol	Customizable pools, DEX aggregation	Best prices, flexibility	May have higher fees due to aggregation

| QuickSwap | Layer-2, low fees | Fast transactions, cost efficiency | Limited to Polygon ecosystem |

DeFi platforms key specifications:

Blockchain: Ethereum, Binance Smart Chain, Solana, or Polygon.

Assets: The types of assets you want to trade or provide liquidity for.

Fees: Transaction fees and potential slippage.

Speed: How quickly you need transactions to be processed.

Additional features: Yield farming, staking, or other services.

Table 4: Platforms: Blockchain, Assets, Speeds, and Features

Platform	BC	Assets	Fees	Speed	Features
Uniswap	ETH	ERC-20 tokens	Moderate fees, potential slippage	Moderate speed	Yield farming, governance
SushiSwap	ETH	ERC-20 tokens	Moderate fees, potential slippage	Moderate speed	Yield farming, staking, MISO
Balancer	ETH	ERC-20 tokens	Moderate fees, potential slippage	Moderate speed	Custom liquidity pools, smart order routing
Curve Finance	ETH	Stablecoins, wrapped assets	Low fees, minimal slippage	Moderate speed	Integration with DeFi ecosystem
Pancake Swap	BSC	BEP-20 tokens	Low fees, fast transactions	High speed	Yield farming, lotteries, NFTs
Bancor	ETH	ERC-20 tokens	Moderate fees, potential slippage	Moderate speed	Impermanent loss protection, single-sided liquidity
Kyber Network	ETH	ERC-20 tokens	Moderate fees, potential slippage	Moderate speed	Liquidity aggregation, integration with dApps
Raydium	SOL	Solana tokens	Low fees, fast transactions	High speed	Integration with Serum, yield farming
1inch Liquidity Protocol	ETH	ERC-20 tokens	Moderate fees, potential slippage	Moderate speed	Customizable pools, DEX aggregation
QuickSwap	MATIC	ERC-20 tokens, Polygon tokens	Low fees, fast transactions	High speed	Yield farming, cross-chain bridges

Hacking and Fraud Incidents Related to AMM Platforms

While the DeFi ecosystem has seen its share of security breaches, many of these platforms have implemented measures to improve their security. It's essential to stay updated on the latest security news and consider the risks involved before investing.

Table 5: Vulnerabilities in Major DeFi Platforms

Platform	Incident	Date	Reference
Uniswap	Flash loan attack	2021	Link
Balancer	Vulnerability exploited	2021	Link
Curve Finance	Vulnerability exploited	2022	Link
Bancor	Smart contract	2018	Link
Kyber Network	Phishing scams	2022	Link
SushiSwap	Phishing scams	2021-23	Link

Technical Aspects

AMM Algorithms: Different AMMs employ various algorithms, such as the constant product formula (Uniswap), constant mean arbitrage (Balancer), and stablecoin-optimized (Curve). Understanding these algorithms helps in evaluating the platform's efficiency and potential for slippage.

Liquidity Pools: Liquidity pools are essential for AMMs to function. Understanding how liquidity is provided, how it's distributed, and the concept of impermanent loss are crucial.

Tokenomics: Many AMMs have their "native tokens", which are often used for governance, incentivizing liquidity providers, and generating revenue. Understanding the "tokenomics" of a platform is essential for evaluating its long-term sustainability and potential returns.

Risk Management

Impermanent Loss: This occurs when the price of an asset in a liquidity pool fluctuates significantly, leading to potential losses compared to holding the assets individually. Understanding impermanent loss and how to mitigate it is crucial for liquidity providers.

DeFi platforms, including AMMs, are susceptible to security vulnerabilities. Staying informed about potential risks and ensuring the platform has robust security measures in place is essential.

User Experience

Interface and Usability: A user-friendly interface with clear instructions and easy navigation is essential for attracting and retaining users.

Understanding the fees charged by the platform and the potential for slippage (the difference between the expected price and the actual price) is key for making informed trading decisions.

Many AMMs integrate with other DeFi protocols, such as lending platforms and yield farming aggregators. Understanding these integrations can enhance the overall user experience and potential returns.

Regulatory Landscape

As the DeFi ecosystem evolves, regulatory frameworks are also developing. Understanding the regulatory landscape and how it may impact AMM platforms is important for long-term viability.

Legal issues such as jurisdiction, taxation, and securities laws can affect AMM platforms.

Automated Market Makers (AMMs) Algorithms

Automated Market Makers (AMMs) revolutionized decentralized trading by eliminating the need for traditional order books and centralized intermediaries. The core innovation of AMMs lies in their pricing algorithms, which determine how assets are traded within liquidity pools. Various AMM algorithms have been developed to provide to different trading needs and asset types, each with its unique formula and characteristics.

This detailed explanation covers the most prominent AMM algorithms used in the DeFi ecosystem:

1. Constant Product Market Maker (CPMM)
2. Constant Sum Market Maker (CSMM)
3. Hybrid Functions (e.g., Curve's StableSwap)
4. Constant Mean Market Maker
5. Proactive Market Maker (PMM)
6. Dynamic Automated Market Maker (DAMM)
7. StableSwap Invariant

Constant Product Market Maker (CPMM)

The Constant Product Market Maker is the most widely used AMM algorithm, popularized by platforms like Uniswap. It enables users to trade between two assets in a liquidity pool while ensuring that the product of the quantities of these assets remains constant.

The fundamental equation governing CPMM is: $x.y = k$

x: Quantity of Asset A in the pool.
y: Quantity of Asset B in the pool.
k: A constant value that remains unchanged during trades (assuming no external liquidity changes).

How It Works:

Liquidity Provision: Liquidity providers (LPs) deposit equal value amounts of two assets into the pool, establishing the initial reserves x and y.

Trading Mechanism:
When a trader wants to swap Asset A for Asset B:
They add a certain amount Δx to the pool.
The pool dispenses an amount Δy of Asset B such that the product
The price of the assets adjusts automatically based on the pool balances.
$(x + \Delta x)(y - \Delta y) = k$
Price Determination:

The current price of Asset A in terms of Asset B is given by P=(y/x) As trades occur, the ratio changes, reflecting the new market price.
Example Calculation:

Suppose:

> Initial pool: 100 ETH and 40,000 USDC (implying ETH price = 400 USDC). Trader wants to buy 10 ETH:

Given:

> Initial Pool Reserves: 100 ETH and 40,000 USDC (implying an initial price of 1 ETH = 400 USDC)

Transaction:

> Trader wants to buy: 10 ETH

CPMM Formula:

Constant Product: $x.y = k$
 where x is the quantity of ETH,
 y is the quantity of USDC
 k is a constant.
Initial Setup:
 x=100 ETH
 y=40,000 USDC
 $x.y = k$ = 4,000,000
After the Trade:

- ETH reserve after the trade (x^i):

x^i=100 ETH−10 ETH=90 ETH

New USDC Reserve Calculation:

Using the constant product formula $k = x^i.y^i$

$$y^i = \frac{k}{x^i} = \frac{4,000,000}{90} = 44,444.44 \; USDC$$

USDC Paid by Trader:

USDC difference

$$y^i - y = 44{,}444.44\ USDC - 40{,}000\ USDC = 4{,}444.44\ USDC$$

Effective Price Per ETH:

$$Price\ per\ ETH = \frac{USDC\ Paid}{ETH\ Bought} = \frac{4{,}444.44}{10} = 444.44\ USDC\ per\ ETH$$

The trader buys 10 ETH for 4,444.44 USDC.

The effective price per ETH has increased to 444.44 USDC (compared to the initial 400 USDC), demonstrating slippage due to the trade's impact on the liquidity pool.

Advantages
    Simplicity: Easy to understand and implement.
    Infinite Liquidity: Theoretically allows for any trade size, though price impact increases with trade size.
    Decentralization: No need for order books or centralized entities.
    Permissionless: Anyone can provide liquidity or trade.

Disadvantages
    Price Slippage: Large trades relative to pool size cause significant price impact.
    Impermanent Loss: LPs may incur losses compared to holding assets due to price fluctuations.
    Inefficiency with Similar-Priced Assets: Not optimal for assets with tightly correlated prices (e.g., stablecoins).

Use Cases
    General Trading: Suitable for trading between volatile and uncorrelated assets.
    Token Launches: Easy setup for new tokens to establish liquidity.

Constant Sum Market Maker (CSMM)

The Constant Sum Market Maker maintains the sum of the reserves as a constant. It is designed to offer zero slippage for trades but suffers from significant drawbacks in terms of arbitrage and liquidity exhaustion.

The governing equation is:

$x + y = k$

- x: Quantity of Asset A.
- y: Quantity of Asset B.
- k: A constant sum maintained throughout trades.

How It Works:

Zero Slippage: For small trades, the exchange rate remains constant, providing perfect pricing.

Arbitrage Vulnerability: If external market prices shift, arbitrageurs can deplete the pool's reserves, leading to potential exhaustion.

Example Calculation:

Suppose:

Initial pool: 100 DAI and 100 USDC, with k=200
Trader wants to swap 10 DAI for USDC:
DAI reserve becomes 110 DAI, and USDC reserve becomes
$$k - 110 \text{ DAI} = 90 \text{ USDC}$$
Exchange rate remains 1:1, with zero slippage.

Advantages
- Zero Slippage: Ideal for identical or pegged assets.
- Simple Pricing: Fixed exchange rates simplify calculations.

Disadvantages
- Liquidity Drainage: Prone to complete depletion of one asset if market prices diverge.
- No Price Discovery: Doesn't adjust to market prices; relies on external parity.

Use Cases
- Identical Assets: Potentially useful for swapping identical tokens but rarely used due to practical limitations.

Hybrid Functions (e.g., Curve's StableSwap)

Hybrid AMM algorithms combine features of constant product and constant sum models to optimize for trading between assets with similar values (e.g., stablecoins), offering low slippage and better capital efficiency. Curve Finance pioneered the StableSwap algorithm, tailored for stablecoins and pegged assets.

The StableSwap formula is complex but can be conceptually understood as:

$$D = n \cdot \prod_{i=1}^{n} x_i + A \cdot \left(\sum_{i=1}^{n} x_i\right)$$

> D: Total invariant representing the pool's combined liquidity.
>
> n: Number of assets in the pool.
>
> x_i: Quantity of each asset.
>
> A: Amplification coefficient adjusting the curvature between constant product and constant sum.

How It Works

Amplification Coefficient (A):

> High A Value: Behaves more like constant sum, offering low slippage for small trades.
>
> Low A Value: Approaches constant product behavior, ensuring stability under larger price deviations.

Dynamic Pricing: The algorithm adjusts pricing based on the current pool balances and the A parameter, maintaining tight spreads and low slippage.

Example Calculation:

Suppose:

> Pool with DAI and USDC, each at 1 million units.
>
> A = 100: High amplification for low slippage.
>
> Trader swaps 100,000 DAI for USDC:

The algorithm calculates minimal change in price, ensuring close to 1:1 exchange with negligible slippage.

Advantages

Low Slippage: Ideal for trading between stablecoins or similarly pegged assets.

Capital Efficiency: Enables large trades with minimal price impact.

Reduced Impermanent Loss: Less exposure to price divergence reduces risk for LPs.

Disadvantages

Complexity: More complicated to understand and implement.

Less Versatile: Optimized specifically for similar-priced assets; not ideal for volatile pairs.

Use Cases

Stablecoin Exchanges: Swapping between different stablecoins (e.g., DAI, USDC, USDT).

Pegged Assets: Trading between assets like wBTC and renBTC.

Constant Mean Market Maker

The Constant Mean Market Maker generalizes the constant product formula by supporting pools with more than two assets and customizable weighting, as implemented by platforms like Balancer.

The generalized formula is:

$$\prod_{i=1}^{n} x_i^{w_i} = k$$

n: Number of assets in the pool.

x_i Quantity of each asset.

w_i: Weighting factor for each asset, where:

$$\sum_{i=1}^{n} w_i = 1$$

k: Constant product maintained across trades.

Multi-Asset Pools: This model allows for the creation of pools containing multiple assets, each assigned a specific weighting. This can include diverse assets such as different cryptocurrencies or tokens.

Flexible Portfolio Management: Liquidity providers (LPs) can utilize these pools to create and manage portfolios that resemble customizable index funds. These pools automatically rebalance based on changes in asset prices, adhering to the predefined asset weights.

Pricing Mechanism: The prices of assets within the pool adjust automatically based on their relative supplies and their specified weights. This mechanism ensures that the pool remains balanced and that asset exchange rates reflect current market dynamics.

Example Calculation:

Suppose:

> Pool with 3 assets: ETH, DAI, and WBTC.
> Weights: 50% ETH, 25% DAI, 25% WBTC.
> Trade: A user swaps DAI for ETH.

The formula adjusts the quantities to maintain the weighted geometric mean constant, ensuring the pool stays balanced according to specified weights.

Advantages
> Diversification: LPs can hold a diversified portfolio within a single pool.
> Automatic Rebalancing: As prices change, the pool rebalances assets, potentially capturing gains.
> Customizable Exposure: Allows for tailored investment strategies through adjustable weights.

Disadvantages
> Complexity: More complex than two-asset AMMs, both in understanding and computation.

Impermanent Loss: Risk persists, especially if asset prices diverge significantly.

Lower Liquidity per Pair: With more assets, liquidity is spread thinner across pairs, potentially increasing slippage.

Use Cases

Index Funds: Creating decentralized index-like funds tracking a basket of assets.

Portfolio Management: Efficient management and rebalancing of diverse crypto portfolios.

Proactive Market Maker (PMM)

The Proactive Market Maker algorithm[10], used by platforms like DODO, aims to improve capital efficiency and reduce impermanent loss by mimicking order book trading behaviors of centralized exchanges[11].

The PMM algorithm adjusts prices proactively based on external price feeds:

$P = P_m \, x \, (1 + k + \Delta Q)$

P: Current price offered by the PMM.
P_m: Market price obtained from an external oracle.
k: A parameter controlling the price sensitivity (liquidity depth).
ΔQ: Quantity deviation from the market equilibrium.

How It Works:

External Price Oracles: The PMM relies on accurate and timely external price feeds to establish baseline market prices, which are essential for the algorithm to function correctly.

Price Adjustments: Prices within the PMM are adjusted proactively in response to trade sizes and prevailing market conditions. This proactive

---

[10] https://docs.dodoex.io/en/product/pmm-algorithm
[11] https://blog.dodoex.io/proactive-market-making-algorithm-a-universal-liquidity-framework-4dec7fae7091

adjustment aims to maintain tighter price spreads and reduce slippage for traders.

Capital Efficiency: The PMM model requires less liquidity to achieve similar or superior market depth compared to traditional Constant Product Market Maker (CPMM) models, thus increasing capital efficiency.

Example Calculation

Suppose:

> External market price for ETH is $3,000.
> $k = 0.01$: Indicates moderate price sensitivity.
> Trade: A user buys 10 ETH.

The PMM adjusts the price slightly above $3,000 based on the trade size and k value, ensuring minimal slippage and maintaining balance.

Advantages
> Reduced Slippage: Offers better prices for traders, especially for large trades.
> Lower Impermanent Loss: Closer tracking of market prices reduces divergence losses for LPs.
> Capital Efficiency: Achieves deep liquidity with less capital compared to traditional AMMs.

Disadvantages
> Reliance on Oracles: Depends heavily on accurate and secure external price feeds; oracle failures can be detrimental.
> Complexity: More sophisticated algorithm requires careful tuning and understanding.
> Centralization Concerns: Oracle dependency may introduce centralization risks.

Use Cases
> High-Volume Trading: Suitable for assets with high trading volumes requiring low slippage.
> Stablecoin and Volatile Asset Pairs: Efficiently handles both stable and volatile asset pairs with appropriate oracle support.

Dynamic Automated Market Maker (DAMM)

Dynamic AMMs adjust their parameters in real-time based on market conditions to optimize trading efficiency and liquidity provision. They aim to balance between minimizing slippage and reducing impermanent loss dynamically.

Implementations

> Kyber Dynamic Market Maker[12] (DMM): Adjusts fee levels based on market volatility.
>
> Variable Curve AMMs: Alter their pricing curves dynamically.

Mathematical Concepts

> Dynamic Fee Adjustment:
>
> High Volatility: Increases fees to compensate LPs for higher risk.
>
> Low Volatility: Decreases fees to encourage trading activity.

How It Works:

Volatility Assessment: The AMM monitors market volatility indicators. Parameter Tuning: Adjusts internal parameters such as fee rates and amplification factors in response. Enhanced Efficiency: Seeks to provide optimal trading conditions across varying market states.

Example Calculation

Suppose:

> Normal Conditions: Trading fee is 0.2%.
> Increased Volatility Detected: Fee adjusts upwards to 0.5% to protect LPs and capture additional earnings.
> Stable Conditions Return: Fee reduces back to 0.2% to promote more trading activity.

---

[12] https://thedefiant.io/news/defi/kyber-launches-dynamic-market-maker-to-optimize-liquidity-provider-fees

Advantages
> Adaptive Performance: Maintains optimal operation across different market conditions.
>
> Improved LP Returns: Dynamically adjusts to protect and enhance liquidity provider earnings.
>
> Flexible Trading Costs: Traders benefit from lower fees during stable periods.

Disadvantages
> Complexity: Implementation and understanding are more difficult.
>
> Potential for Instability: Incorrect parameter adjustments could lead to inefficiencies.
>
> Reliance on Accurate Metrics: Requires precise and timely market data for effective adjustments.

Use Cases
> Volatile Markets: Suitable for assets with fluctuating volatility profiles.
>
> High-Frequency Trading: Benefits scenarios where market conditions change rapidly.

StableSwap Invariant (Advanced Implementations)

Advanced versions of stable swap algorithms further optimize for minimal slippage and impermanent loss across a broader range of price movements and asset types.

Implementations
> Saddle Finance[13]: An AMM focused on efficient stablecoin and pegged asset swaps using an optimized StableSwap algorithm.
>
> Shell Protocol[14]: Utilizes advanced mathematical models to improve liquidity and pricing efficiency.

Mathematical Concepts:

---

[13] https://www.saddle.finance
[14] https://docs.shellprotocol.io

Advanced Curvature Adjustments: Fine-tunes the balance between constant sum and constant product behaviors over different price ranges. Liquidity Redistribution: Dynamically allocates liquidity where it's most needed based on trading patterns.

How It Works:

Enhanced Flexibility: Allows for efficient swaps even when asset prices deviate slightly from their peg. Risk Mitigation: Incorporates mechanisms to protect LPs from losses during extreme market conditions.

Advantages
> Ultra-Low Slippage: Facilitates large volume trades with negligible price impact.
> Resilience: Better withstands market stress and price deviations.
> LP Protection: Reduces risk exposure for liquidity providers.

Disadvantages
> High Complexity: Very intricate models that require deep understanding and precise implementation.
> Limited Asset Scope: Primarily effective for stable or tightly correlated assets.

Use Cases
> Cross-Chain Assets: Efficient swapping between assets pegged across different chains.
> Advanced DeFi Applications: Underpinning complex financial products requiring stable and efficient asset exchanges.

Liquidity-Sensitive AMM (LS-AMM)

The Liquidity-Sensitive AMM[15] is designed to address the issue of low liquidity in certain pools by dynamically adjusting prices based on the liquidity depth. This model is particularly useful in situations where there is significant variation in liquidity across different trading pairs or during different market conditions.

---

[15] https://www.eecs.harvard.edu/cs286r/courses/fall12/papers/OPRS10.pdf

The pricing mechanism in LS-AMM can be generalized as:

$$P = P_m x (1 + \frac{\Delta Q}{L})$$

P: Current price offered by the AMM.
P_m: Market price derived from an external source or previous trades.
ΔQ: Quantity of the asset being traded.
L: Liquidity depth in the pool.

How It Works:

Dynamic Pricing Adjustment: The algorithm adjusts the price more sensitively in pools with lower liquidity, preventing drastic price changes and making the trading process more efficient.

Liquidity Monitoring: LS-AMM continuously monitors the liquidity in the pool and adapts the price curve to reflect the current state of liquidity, reducing slippage for traders and improving the stability of the pool.

Advantages
  Enhanced Efficiency in Low Liquidity Pools: Improves trading outcomes in pools with varying liquidity levels, making them more attractive to traders.
  Reduced Slippage: By adjusting prices based on liquidity depth, LS-AMM reduces slippage, particularly in less liquid markets.

Disadvantages
  Complexity: Requires careful calibration to ensure accurate liquidity-sensitive pricing, which can be more complex than simpler AMM models.
  Dependence on Accurate Liquidity Metrics: Effectiveness hinges on the accuracy and timeliness of liquidity data.

Use Cases
  Niche Market Pairs: Suitable for trading pairs with lower liquidity or those that experience fluctuating liquidity conditions.
  Emerging Markets: Ideal for newly launched tokens or markets where liquidity has not yet stabilized.

Order Book Hybrid AMM

Order Book Hybrid AMMs[16] combine the benefits of traditional order book exchanges with AMM models, aiming to offer deep liquidity, efficient pricing, and reduced slippage. This hybrid approach allows the platform to provide more flexible trading options, accommodating both market makers and liquidity providers.

How It Works:

Order Book Integration: The platform maintains an order book that works alongside the AMM, allowing users to place limit orders or trade directly with the liquidity pool.

Dynamic Market Making: The algorithm dynamically adjusts the AMM's pricing based on the state of the order book, ensuring that prices remain competitive with those available through limit orders.

Price Discovery: The combination of order book and AMM facilitates better price discovery, especially in markets with low liquidity or high volatility.

Advantages
>   Enhanced Price Discovery: Offers more accurate pricing by incorporating both AMM-based trades and order book data.
>   Flexible Trading: Traders can choose between using the AMM or placing orders on the order book, depending on their strategy.
>   Improved Liquidity: By combining liquidity from both AMM pools and order books, the platform can provide deeper liquidity, especially for large trades.

Disadvantages
>   Increased Complexity: The hybrid model is more complex to implement and use, requiring traders and liquidity providers to understand both systems.

---

[16] https://docs.vertexprotocol.com/basics/technical-architecture

Potential Fragmentation: Liquidity might be split between the AMM and order book, potentially leading to inefficiencies if not managed correctly.

Use Cases

High-Volume Trading: Suitable for assets with high trading volumes where price precision is crucial.

Sophisticated Traders: Appeals to users who are familiar with traditional order books and want the added benefits of AMMs.

Multi-Curve AMM

Multi-Curve AMMs[17] utilize multiple pricing curves[18] within a single liquidity pool to handle trades across different ranges of liquidity or price volatility. This approach allows for more efficient trading across a wide range of market conditions and asset types.

The Multi-Curve model can be described as:

$$P = \sum_{i=1}^{n} f_i(x,y,z)$$

P: Composite price derived from multiple curves.

f_i: Individual pricing functions representing different liquidity or volatility scenarios.

x, y, z: Quantities of assets in the pool or other parameters influencing pricing.

How It Works:

Composite Pricing: The Multi-Curve AMM uses a summation of different pricing functions (f_i) to calculate a comprehensive price that reflects varied trading conditions within the same pool. This allows the AMM to dynamically adjust to changes in liquidity, volatility, or other market dynamics.

Individual Curves: Each function f_i is tailored to specific aspects of market behavior, such as high liquidity trading periods or high volatility

---

[17] https://docs.planar.finance/protocol-components/multi-curve-amm
[18] https://www.gemini.com/cryptopedia/curve-crypto-automated-market-maker

scenarios, allowing the AMM to handle trades more effectively across a spectrum of conditions.

Flexibility in Parameters: The variables "x,y,z" represent the asset quantities or other relevant parameters that affect the pricing curves, providing the flexibility needed to adapt to different trading strategies and pool compositions.

Advantages
> Versatility: Handles a wide range of market conditions and asset types, providing efficient pricing across various scenarios.
> Optimized Slippage: Reduces slippage by matching trades to the most appropriate pricing curve for the current market condition.
> Improved Risk Management: By diversifying pricing mechanisms, the Multi-Curve AMM mitigates risks associated with using a single curve model.

Disadvantages
> Complexity: Requires sophisticated algorithms and greater computational resources to manage multiple curves effectively.
> Implementation Challenges: Developing and maintaining the system can be more resource-intensive compared to simpler AMMs.

Use Cases
> Volatile Markets: Ideal for assets with varying degrees of volatility, where different pricing mechanisms might be needed depending on market conditions.
> Diverse Asset Pools: Suitable for liquidity pools containing assets with different risk profiles and liquidity needs.

Oracle-Based AMM

Oracle-Based AMMs[19] rely heavily on external data sources (oracles) to adjust prices within the AMM, ensuring that the prices reflect real-time market conditions more accurately. This model is particularly useful for maintaining price stability and reducing arbitrage opportunities.

---

[19] https://medium.com/@yieldops/comparing-defi-market-makers-from-amms-to-oracle-based-innovations-c7527d8e8e4e

How It Works

> External Price Feeds: The AMM uses oracles to obtain real-time market prices for assets, which are then used to adjust the internal pricing within the liquidity pool.
>
> Dynamic Price Adjustment: Prices within the AMM are continually adjusted to match those provided by the oracles, reducing the likelihood of significant price deviations.
>
> Arbitrage Mitigation: By keeping prices closely aligned with external markets, the AMM reduces the potential for arbitrage, ensuring that liquidity providers are less exposed to impermanent loss.

Advantages

> Accurate Pricing: Ensures that the AMM's prices are in line with the broader market, reducing slippage and improving trading efficiency.
>
> Lower Impermanent Loss: By aligning closely with external prices, LPs face less risk of impermanent loss due to price discrepancies.
>
> Arbitrage Resistance: Reduces the profitability of arbitrage, keeping the liquidity pool more stable.

Disadvantages

> Oracle Dependency: Relies on the accuracy and security of oracles, which can be a single point of failure.
>
> Centralization Concerns: Depending on the oracle provider, the system might introduce a degree of centralization, contrary to the philosophy of decentralization in DeFi.

Use Cases

> Stablecoin Trading: Ideal for pools involving stablecoins or other pegged assets, where price accuracy is critical.
>
> High-Volume Assets: Useful for assets with significant external market data, ensuring that the AMM's pricing remains competitive and accurate.

Time-Weighted Average Price (TWAP) AMM

TWAP AMMs[20] utilize time-weighted average prices to smooth out volatility and reduce the impact of short-term price fluctuations. This approach is particularly useful for larger trades that might otherwise experience significant slippage in more volatile markets.

How It Works

Time Averaging: The AMM calculates prices based on the average over a set period, rather than using the current spot price. This smooths out short-term volatility and provides a more stable price for traders.

Price Stability: By reducing the impact of sudden price changes, TWAP AMMs help mitigate the effects of market manipulation or flash crashes.

Advantages
> Reduced Slippage: Larger trades benefit from the averaging mechanism, which reduces slippage by spreading the price impact over time.
> Price Stability: Helps maintain more stable prices within the AMM, making it more attractive for long-term traders and liquidity providers.
> Market Integrity: By minimizing the impact of short-term price fluctuations, TWAP AMMs contribute to overall market stability.

Disadvantages
> Lag in Price Response: In rapidly changing markets, TWAP AMMs may lag in responding to new price levels, potentially leading to arbitrage opportunities.
> Complexity: Implementing time-weighted pricing adds complexity to the AMM, both in terms of computation and user understanding.

Use Cases
> Large Institutional Trades: Ideal for institutional or large-scale traders looking to execute big orders with minimal slippage.
> Volatile Markets: Useful in markets prone to short-term volatility, providing a more stable trading environment.

---

[20] https://chain.link/education-hub/twap-vs-vwap

Continuous Function Market Makers (CFMMs)

Continuous Function Market Makers[21] are a generalization of AMMs, where the pricing mechanism is determined by a continuous mathematical function. This category includes various AMM designs, such as the Constant Product, Constant Mean, and others, but can also incorporate more complex functions tailored to specific trading needs.

The general formula for CFMMs is:

$$f(x_1, x_2, \dots x_n) = k$$

> f: A continuous function representing the relationship between the quantities of different assets in the pool.
> $x\_1, x\_2, \dots, x\_n$: Quantities of the assets in the pool.
> k: A constant that the function maintains during trades.

Flexible Pricing Functions: CFMMs are designed to adapt to a wide range of asset types and market conditions by allowing the use of different mathematical functions as pricing mechanisms. This flexibility supports more complex trading dynamics and caters to diverse liquidity needs. Liquidity providers can choose or design functions that align with their risk-return preferences. This customization is crucial in markets where asset behaviors vary significantly or where advanced trading strategies are implemented.

Advantages
> Versatility: Supports a broad range of asset types and trading strategies, from simple to highly complex.
> Customizable Risk Profile: Liquidity providers can adjust the function to manage their exposure to different types of risk, such as impermanent loss or slippage.
> Enhanced Efficiency: Optimizes trading outcomes across diverse market conditions.

Disadvantages
> Complexity: Designing and implementing a CFMM requires advanced mathematical and financial knowledge.

---

[21] https://eprint.iacr.org/2021/1101.pdf

Computational Intensity: More complex functions may require significant computational resources, potentially increasing gas costs.

Use Cases

Advanced Financial Products: Suitable for building sophisticated financial products that require customized pricing mechanisms.

Dynamic Trading Environments: Ideal for environments where trading conditions change rapidly and require adaptable AMM mechanisms.

Rebalancing AMM

Rebalancing AMMs are designed to automatically rebalance the asset ratios within the pool based on predefined criteria, such as market conditions, asset volatility, or user preferences. This rebalancing can help maintain optimal liquidity and reduce the risk of impermanent loss.

Automatic Rebalancing: The AMM algorithm periodically or continuously adjusts the asset ratios in the pool to maintain a balanced portfolio, according to the defined strategy.

Dynamic Liquidity Management: Rebalancing helps optimize the pool's liquidity distribution, ensuring that no single asset becomes too dominant or too scarce.

Advantages

Optimized Portfolio Management: Helps maintain a balanced asset allocation, reducing risk and improving returns for liquidity providers.

Lower Impermanent Loss: By keeping asset ratios balanced, rebalancing AMMs can reduce the impact of price fluctuations on LPs.

Disadvantages

Higher Transaction Costs: Frequent rebalancing can lead to increased transaction costs, particularly on networks with high gas fees.

Complexity in Implementation: Requires careful design and management to ensure that rebalancing strategies are effective and do not introduce additional risks.

Use Cases

Portfolio Diversification: Ideal for liquidity pools that aim to maintain a diversified portfolio of assets.

Long-Term Investments: Suitable for long-term liquidity providers who want to minimize risk while earning steady returns.

Structured AMM (SAMM)

Structured AMMs combine features of traditional financial derivatives (such as options or futures) with AMM principles to offer more complex and customizable financial products. These AMMs are designed to provide to users with complex trading strategies and risk management needs.

How It Works:

Integration of Derivatives: SAMMs incorporate derivative-like features, such as options pricing models, into the AMM framework, allowing for more complex trading scenarios.

Customizable Parameters: Users can adjust parameters such as strike prices, expiration dates, or volatility assumptions to tailor the AMM's behavior to their specific needs.

Advantages

Advanced Financial Instruments: Enables the creation of structured financial products within a decentralized framework, expanding the range of available DeFi tools.

Customizable Risk Management: Users can fine-tune their exposure to different types of risk, offering greater control over their investments.

Disadvantages

Complexity: Requires a deep understanding of both AMM mechanisms and financial derivatives, making it less accessible to ordinary users.

> Higher Risk: The integration of derivative features can introduce additional risks, particularly in volatile markets.

Use Cases
> Sophisticated Traders: Appeals to users with advanced knowledge of financial markets who seek to implement complex trading strategies.
>
> Hedging and Speculation: Suitable for users looking to hedge against specific risks or speculate on future price movements using structured products.

Stochastic AMM (S-AMM)

Stochastic AMMs[22] introduce randomness into the pricing mechanism to simulate real-world market behaviors more accurately. This approach helps in preventing certain types of manipulation and can be used to model more complex financial systems within an AMM framework.

Randomized Pricing: The pricing formula in a Stochastic AMM includes a stochastic element, meaning that the price of the assets within the pool fluctuates based on a probability distribution, rather than following a deterministic path.

Market Simulation: By introducing randomness, S-AMMs can better simulate the unpredictability of real markets, which can be particularly useful in testing new financial products or strategies in a decentralized environment.

Advantages
> Anti-Manipulation: The randomness in pricing can make it more difficult for traders to manipulate the market, as the outcomes are not entirely predictable.
>
> Realistic Market Modeling: S-AMMs can be used to model complex financial products that need to account for randomness and uncertainty, providing a more realistic simulation of traditional markets.

---

[22]https://mirror.xyz/hashcurvekris.eth/_0rBy2F2xadg2im6LfprQi5LJ6uh xjHpJm152C_4w6Y

Disadvantages
> Complexity: The introduction of stochastic processes makes the AMM more complex to understand and use, which could be a barrier for ordinary users.
>
> Unpredictable Outcomes: The randomness inherent in the pricing can lead to unpredictable trading outcomes, which may deter users who prefer more stable, deterministic systems.

Use Cases
> Experimental Financial Products: Suitable for DeFi platforms experimenting with new financial products that require a realistic market simulation.
>
> Anti-Manipulation Measures: Ideal for markets where manipulation is a concern and where introducing uncertainty can help deter such behavior.

Composable AMM (C-AMM)

Composable[23] AMMs[24] are designed to interact seamlessly with other DeFi protocols, enabling the creation of complex financial products by combining different DeFi building blocks. These AMMs are modular, allowing for integration with lending platforms, synthetic assets, and other decentralized applications (dApps).

Modularity: C-AMMs are built with modular components that can be easily integrated into other DeFi protocols. For example, a C-AMM might be used as part of a larger protocol that includes lending, borrowing, and trading all within one ecosystem.

Interoperability: These AMMs are designed to be interoperable with other DeFi protocols, allowing liquidity to flow freely between different dApps and enabling more complex financial operations, such as automated yield farming strategies.

Advantages

---

[23] https://medium.com/liveplexmetaverseecosystem/composable-finance-building-blocks-for-the-next-wave-of-defi-2e0ba601e917
[24] https://par.nsf.gov/servlets/purl/10300608

> Enhanced Flexibility: Users can create customized financial products by combining the C-AMM with other DeFi building blocks, offering greater flexibility and innovation.
>
> Interoperability: Facilitates seamless integration with other DeFi protocols, enhancing the overall functionality of the DeFi ecosystem.

Disadvantages

> Complexity: The composable nature of these AMMs can add layers of complexity, particularly when integrating multiple protocols.
>
> Security Risks: The interconnectedness of various DeFi protocols increases the risk of cascading failures if one component is compromised.

Use Cases

> Advanced DeFi Strategies: Suitable for users looking to implement sophisticated strategies that involve multiple DeFi protocols.
>
> Integrated Financial Products: Ideal for creating new financial products that require the combination of trading, lending, and other financial services.

Elastic AMM (E-AMM)

Elastic AMMs[25] adjust their liquidity provision dynamically based on market conditions, trading volume, and asset volatility. This approach aims to optimize the use of liquidity in the pool, reducing slippage and impermanent loss during periods of high volatility.

Dynamic Liquidity Adjustment: The E-AMM algorithm increases or decreases the liquidity available for trading based on real-time market conditions. For example, during periods of high volatility, the E-AMM may allocate more liquidity to reduce slippage.

Volatility Sensitivity: E-AMMs are designed to be sensitive to changes in market volatility, allowing them to respond more effectively to sudden market shifts.

Advantages

---

[25] https://learn.bybit.com/defi/what-is-apex-protocol/

Improved Capital Efficiency: By adjusting liquidity provision dynamically, E-AMMs make more efficient use of the available capital, reducing the need for large static reserves.

Reduced Impermanent Loss: The algorithm's ability to adapt to changing market conditions helps mitigate the impact of impermanent loss for liquidity providers.

Disadvantages

Complexity: The dynamic nature of E-AMMs requires more sophisticated algorithms, which can be complex to develop and implement.

Potential Instability: Rapid adjustments to liquidity could lead to instability in the pricing mechanism if not managed carefully.

Use Cases

High-Volatility Assets: Suitable for trading pairs that experience significant volatility, where dynamic liquidity adjustments can help maintain stable prices.

Adaptive Trading Environments: Ideal for DeFi platforms that need to adapt quickly to changing market conditions.

Pareto-Optimal AMM

Pareto-Optimal AMMs are designed to optimize[26] the allocation of liquidity in a way that no individual liquidity provider can be made better off without making another worse off. This concept, borrowed from economics, ensures that the AMM operates in the most efficient manner possible, given the constraints.

Pareto Efficiency: The AMM algorithm continuously adjusts the allocation of liquidity and pricing to achieve a state where no LP can improve their situation (in terms of returns or risk) without harming another LP. This ensures that the pool operates at maximum efficiency.

Utility Maximization: The AMM also aims to maximize the overall utility for all participants, balancing between optimal returns for LPs and fair pricing for traders.

---

[26] https://ideas.repec.org/p/arx/papers/2402.09129.html

Advantages
> Optimal Liquidity Distribution: Ensures that liquidity is distributed in the most efficient manner, reducing waste and improving returns for all LPs.
>
> Fairness: The Pareto-optimal approach promotes fairness among liquidity providers, as it prevents any one provider from dominating the pool to the detriment of others.

Disadvantages
> Complexity: Achieving Pareto efficiency requires advanced mathematical models and can be computationally intensive.
>
> Implementation Challenges: Balancing the needs of all participants in the pool can be challenging, particularly in volatile markets.

Use Cases
> Equitable Liquidity Provision: Suitable for pools where fairness among LPs is a priority, ensuring that no participant is unfairly disadvantaged.
>
> Efficient Capital Allocation: Ideal for scenarios where capital efficiency is crucial, such as in pools with limited liquidity.

Machine Learning-Driven AMM

Machine Learning-Driven AMMs[27] utilize machine learning (ML) algorithms to optimize trading strategies, pricing mechanisms, and liquidity provision dynamically. These AMMs learn from historical data and adjust their parameters in real-time to maximize efficiency and returns.

How It Works:

Data-Driven Decision Making: The ML algorithms analyze large datasets, including historical trades, market conditions, and external factors, to predict future price movements and optimize the AMM's behavior accordingly.

---

[27] https://jfin-swufe.springeropen.com/articles/10.1186/s40854-024-00660-0

Adaptive Algorithms: The AMM continually updates its models based on new data, allowing it to adapt to changing market conditions and improve its performance over time.

Advantages

> Improved Predictive Accuracy: By leveraging machine learning, these AMMs can make more accurate predictions about price movements, leading to better pricing and reduced slippage.
>
> Dynamic Optimization: The ability to adapt and learn from new data allows these AMMs to continuously improve their efficiency, offering better outcomes for both traders and LPs.

Disadvantages

> Complexity and Resource Intensive: Implementing ML-driven AMMs requires significant computational resources and expertise in both machine learning and finance.
>
> Data Dependency: The effectiveness of the AMM is heavily dependent on the quality and quantity of the data it receives, which can be a limiting factor.

Use Cases

> High-Frequency Trading: Suitable for environments where quick, accurate predictions are crucial, such as in high-frequency trading scenarios.
>
> Complex Financial Products: Ideal for DeFi platforms offering advanced financial products that require sophisticated pricing mechanisms.

A summary of the advantages, disadvantages, and typical use cases of the selected algorithms is provided in Table 15.

Table 6: Automated MMA: Advantages, Disadvantages, Use Cases

AMM Algorithm	Advantages	Disadvantages	Use Cases
Constant Product Market Maker (CPMM)	Simplicity, infinite liquidity, decentralization	Price slippage, impermanent loss, inefficient for similar-priced assets	General trading, token launches
Constant Sum Market Maker (CSMM)	Zero slippage, simple pricing	Liquidity drainage, no price discovery	Identical assets swapping (rarely used)

Hybrid Functions (Curve's StableSwap)	Low slippage, capital efficiency, reduced impermanent loss	Complexity, less versatile	Stablecoin exchanges, pegged assets trading
Constant Mean Market Maker	Diversification, automatic rebalancing, customizable exposure	Complexity, impermanent loss, lower liquidity per pair	Index funds, portfolio management
Proactive Market Maker (PMM)	Reduced slippage, lower impermanent loss, capital efficiency	Reliance on oracles, complexity, centralization concerns	High-volume trading, stablecoin and volatile asset pairs
Dynamic Automated Market Maker (DAMM)	Adaptive performance, improved LP returns, flexible trading costs	Complexity, potential instability, reliance on accurate metrics	Volatile markets, high-frequency trading
StableSwap Invariant (Advanced Implementations)	Ultra-low slippage, resilience, LP protection	High complexity, limited asset scope	Cross-chain assets, advanced DeFi applications
Liquidity-Sensitive AMM (LS-AMM)	Enhanced efficiency in low liquidity pools, reduced slippage	Complexity, dependence on accurate liquidity metrics	Niche market pairs, emerging markets
Order Book Hybrid AMM	Enhanced price discovery, flexible trading, improved liquidity	Increased complexity, potential fragmentation	High-volume trading, sophisticated traders
Multi-Curve AMM	Versatility, optimized slippage, improved risk management	Complexity, implementation challenges	Volatile markets, diverse asset pools
Oracle-Based AMM	Accurate pricing, lower impermanent loss, arbitrage resistance	Oracle dependency, centralization concerns	Stablecoin trading, high-volume assets
Time-Weighted Average Price (TWAP) AMM	Reduced slippage, price stability, market integrity	Lag in price response, complexity	Large institutional trades, volatile markets
Continuous	Versatility,	Complexity,	Advanced

Function Market Makers (CFMMs)	customizable risk profile, enhanced efficiency	computational intensity	financial products, dynamic trading environments
Rebalancing AMM	Optimized portfolio management, lower impermanent loss	Higher transaction costs, complexity in implementation	Portfolio diversification, long-term investments
Structured AMM (SAMM)	Advanced financial instruments, customizable risk management	Complexity, higher risk	Sophisticated traders, hedging and speculation
Stochastic AMM (S-AMM)	Anti-manipulation, realistic market modeling	Complexity, unpredictable outcomes	Experimental financial products, anti-manipulation measures
Composable AMM (C-AMM)	Enhanced flexibility, interoperability, innovative financial products	Complexity, security risks	Advanced DeFi strategies, integrated financial products
Elastic AMM (E-AMM)	Improved capital efficiency, reduced impermanent loss	Complexity, potential instability	High-volatility assets, adaptive trading environments
Pareto-Optimal AMM	Optimal liquidity distribution, fairness, efficient capital allocation	Complexity, implementation challenges	Equitable liquidity provision, efficient capital allocation
Machine Learning-Driven AMM	Improved predictive accuracy, dynamic optimization	Complexity, resource-intensive, data dependency	High-frequency trading, complex financial products

Popular Platforms: There are around 20-30 widely recognized and actively used AMMs spread across major blockchains. Total AMMs: Including smaller, emerging, and specialized platforms, the number could easily be over 100 AMMs in active use today (2024).

Traditional market maker and an Automated Market Maker

The difference between a traditional financial market maker and an Automated Market Maker (AMM) in the context of decentralized finance (DeFi) lies in their operational mechanisms, roles, and the environments in which they function. Below is a detailed comparison of the two mechanisms:

Traditional Financial Market Maker:

Human or Algorithmic Agents: Traditional market makers are typically financial institutions or individual traders who actively quote buy (bid) and sell (ask) prices for financial instruments such as stocks, bonds, options, or currencies.

Profit Mechanism: They profit from the spread between the bid and ask prices, and their role is to provide liquidity to the markets, ensuring that buyers and sellers can trade smoothly.

Order Book-Based: Market makers operate within an order book system, where they continuously provide liquidity by placing buy and sell orders. The order book lists all buy and sell orders, and trades are matched based on these orders.

Active Management: Market makers continuously adjust their prices and the volume of assets they are willing to trade based on market conditions, news, and other factors. This requires active management and decision-making.

Automated Market Maker (AMM):

Decentralized Smart Contracts: AMMs are decentralized protocols that use smart contracts to enable automated trading of assets on blockchain platforms. They remove the need for traditional order books.

Liquidity Pools: Instead of relying on human traders, AMMs use liquidity pools where users (liquidity providers) deposit pairs of assets. The AMM then uses a predefined algorithm to price assets and facilitate trades directly with the liquidity pool.

Passive Liquidity Provision: Liquidity providers earn a portion of the trading fees generated by the pool. They do not actively manage their positions; instead, the AMM's algorithm automatically adjusts prices and executes trades.

Algorithm-Driven: AMMs rely on algorithms (like the constant product formula used by Uniswap) to determine asset prices and execute trades. These algorithms ensure that trading can happen continuously, without the need for active human intervention.

Table 7: Traditional Financial MM and Automated MM

Feature	Traditional Financial Market Maker	Automated Market Maker (AMM)
Agents	Human or Algorithmic Agents	Decentralized Smart Contracts
Profit Mechanism	Spread between bid and ask prices	Liquidity Provider Fees
Order Book	Order-Based	Liquidity Pools
Liquidity Provision	Active Management	Passive Liquidity Provision
Price Determination	Active Management	Algorithm-Driven
Trading Execution	Human or Algorithmic	Algorithmic

Pricing Mechanism

Traditional Financial Market Maker: Bid-Ask Spread: Market makers provide liquidity by quoting both a buy price (bid) and a sell price (ask) for a particular asset. The difference between these prices (the spread) is the market maker's profit margin.

Price Discovery: Prices in traditional markets are determined by supply and demand dynamics, influenced by the market maker's pricing strategy and the order flow from traders. Market makers actively adjust their prices in response to changes in market conditions, aiming to maintain a balanced inventory of assets.

Automated Market Maker (AMM):
Mathematical Formulas: AMMs use mathematical formulas to price assets. The most common formula, the constant product formula $x * y = k$, ensures that the product of the quantities of two assets in a liquidity pool

remains constant. This creates a dynamic pricing model based on the relative supply of the assets in the pool.

No Order Book: AMMs do not have an order book; instead, the price is determined algorithmically by the ratio of assets in the pool. As trades occur, the ratio changes, and so does the price. This mechanism allows for continuous trading without the need for a counterparty.

Liquidity Provision

Traditional Financial Market Maker:
Capital Requirements: Market makers are often required to maintain significant capital reserves to provide liquidity and manage the risk associated with holding large positions in various assets.

Market Maker Obligations: In many cases, especially in regulated markets, market makers have obligations to maintain certain levels of liquidity, even during periods of high volatility.

Automated Market Maker (AMM):
Crowdsourced Liquidity: In AMMs, liquidity is provided by a broad base of users who deposit their assets into liquidity pools. These users earn a portion of the trading fees as a reward for their contribution.

Risk of Impermanent Loss: Liquidity providers in AMMs are exposed to the risk of impermanent loss, which occurs when the price of the deposited assets changes relative to when they were added to the pool. This risk is specific to AMMs and can result in lower returns than holding the assets outside the pool.

Environment and Application

Traditional Financial Market Maker:
Centralized Exchanges: Traditional market makers operate on centralized exchanges (CEXs) and over-the-counter (OTC) markets, which are regulated and operate within specific jurisdictions.
Regulatory Oversight: Market makers are subject to regulatory oversight and are often required to adhere to specific rules and guidelines set by financial regulators.

Automated Market Maker:

Decentralized Exchanges (DEXs): AMMs are integral to decentralized exchanges (DEXs) like Uniswap, SushiSwap, and PancakeSwap, which operate on blockchain networks such as Ethereum, Binance Smart Chain, and Solana.

Lack of Central Authority: AMMs operate without a central authority, relying on smart contracts to enforce rules and execute trades automatically. This decentralization offers greater accessibility but also comes with the risks associated with the blockchain, such as smart contract vulnerabilities and lack of regulatory protections.

Risks and Challenges

Traditional Financial Market Maker:
Inventory Risk: Market makers bear the risk of holding large positions in assets whose prices can fluctuate, potentially leading to losses if market conditions move against their inventory.

Market Manipulation Risk: Market makers need to be cautious of large trades that can significantly move prices, as they can lead to adverse selection and potential losses.

Automated Market Maker (AMM):
AMMs expose liquidity providers to impermanent loss, a unique risk where changes in asset prices can lead to reduced returns.

AMMs are vulnerable to bugs or exploits in their smart contracts. A failure in the contract code can lead to significant losses for users. Also, in low-liquidity pools, large trades can result in significant effect where the execution price deviates substantially from the expected price.

Table 8: Traditional Financial Market Maker vs Automated MM

Aspect	Traditional Financial Market Maker	Automated Market Maker (AMM)
Role	Provides liquidity by quoting bid-ask prices, often actively managed	Provides liquidity through automated algorithms and liquidity pools
Pricing Mechanism	Bid-ask spread, price discovery via order book	Algorithm-driven, no order book, prices set by asset ratios in pools
Liquidity Provision	Requires significant capital, subject to regulatory	Crowdsourced from users, subject to impermanent loss

		obligations
Environment	Operates in centralized, regulated exchanges	Operates in decentralized, unregulated environments on blockchain
Risks	Inventory risk, market manipulation risk	Impermanent loss, smart contract risk, slippage in low-liquidity pools
Regulation	Subject to strict regulatory oversight	Operates in a largely unregulated environment

Machine Learning-Driven Automated Market Makers

Machine Learning-Driven Automated Market Makers (ML-AMMs) represent an advanced and innovative evolution of traditional AMM models. By integrating machine learning (ML) algorithms into the core functioning of AMMs, these systems aim to enhance decision-making processes, optimize trading efficiency, and better manage risks in decentralized finance (DeFi) environments.

Key Concepts and Components of ML-AMMs

ML-AMMs utilize various types of machine learning algorithms to analyze historical and real-time data. These algorithms can include supervised and unsupervised learning, reinforcement learning, and more. The algorithms process large datasets, including historical price data, trading volumes, market volatility, order flow, external news, and on-chain data like wallet activities and transaction patterns.

Unlike traditional AMMs that use static formulas (e.g., constant product formula), ML-AMMs employ dynamic pricing models that adjust based on market conditions. These models predict future price movements and adjust the AMM's parameters to optimize trading outcomes. ML-AMMs continuously monitor market conditions and can adjust liquidity provision, slippage tolerance, and trading fees in real-time to reflect current market realities.

Machine learning models can predict market volatility more accurately than traditional methods, allowing ML-AMMs to adjust their operations to mitigate risks such as impermanent loss. ML-AMMs can deploy risk mitigation strategies like hedging, rebalancing, or dynamic liquidity adjustment based on predictive analytics, reducing the exposure of liquidity providers to market risks.

By predicting market trends and user behavior, ML-AMMs can optimize liquidity distribution across different pools, ensuring that capital is used more efficiently and that pools are better equipped to handle large trades without significant slippage. ML-AMMs can automatically adjust liquidity levels based on market demand, providing more liquidity during high trading volumes and reducing it during low activity periods to prevent capital inefficiency.

ML-AMMs continuously "learn" from market outcomes and user interactions. The algorithms refine their strategies over time, improving the accuracy of their predictions and the efficiency of their operations. The AMM can adapt its strategy in real-time, responding to sudden market changes, such as a spike in volatility, ensuring that the system remains robust and effective under various conditions.

Types of Machine Learning Models Used in ML-AMMs

Supervised Learning:

Supervised learning models[28] are trained on labeled historical data to predict future outcomes, such as asset prices or volatility levels. These predictions help the AMM adjust its pricing and liquidity strategies.
Examples: Linear regression, decision trees, and neural networks are common supervised learning models used in financial forecasting.

Unsupervised Learning:

Unsupervised learning models[29] detect patterns or anomalies in the data without prior labeling. These models can identify emerging trends or market anomalies that may not be immediately apparent.
Examples: Clustering algorithms like k-means[30] or hierarchical clustering can group similar market behaviors, aiding in the identification of trading patterns or market segmentation.

Reinforcement Learning:

---

[28] https://www.ibm.com/topics/supervised-learning
[29] https://www.ibm.com/topics/unsupervised-learning
[30] https://www.ibm.com/topics/k-means-clustering

Reinforcement learning models optimize decision-making by learning through trial and error, adjusting strategies based on the outcomes of past actions. This approach is particularly useful in environments with complex, dynamic interactions like DeFi markets.

Examples: "Q-learning" and "deep reinforcement learning" are used to develop adaptive trading strategies that evolve based on market feedback.

Deep Learning:

Complex Pattern Recognition: Deep learning models, such as convolutional neural networks (CNNs) or recurrent neural networks (RNNs), can process and learn from large, complex datasets. They are particularly effective in identifying intricate patterns and trends in financial data.

Applications: Deep learning can be applied to time-series forecasting, sentiment analysis from social media, and real-time market prediction.

Advantages of Machine Learning Models

Enhanced Pricing Efficiency: By leveraging machine learning, ML-AMMs can make more accurate predictions about price movements and market conditions, leading to better pricing and reduced slippage.

Informed Decision-Making: The ability to process vast amounts of data allows ML-AMMs to make more informed decisions, optimizing trading and liquidity provision.

Real-Time Adaptation: ML-AMMs can adapt their parameters in real-time based on market conditions, providing a more responsive and efficient trading environment.

Continuous Improvement: As ML models learn and evolve, the AMM becomes increasingly efficient, refining its strategies to improve performance over time.

Predictive Risk Mitigation: By accurately predicting market volatility and other risk factors, ML-AMMs can proactively implement risk management strategies, reducing the potential for impermanent loss and other financial risks.

Volatility Control: Adaptive strategies allow ML-AMMs to manage liquidity and pricing in response to market volatility, ensuring stable and predictable outcomes for users.

Optimized Liquidity Allocation: Machine learning enables more efficient use of capital, as the AMM can dynamically allocate liquidity to where it is most needed, reducing the waste of resources and improving returns for liquidity providers.

Adaptive Fee Structures: ML-AMMs can adjust fee structures based on predicted trading volumes and market conditions, ensuring that fees are competitive while maximizing profitability.

Disadvantages and Challenges of ML-AMMs

Implementation Complexity: Developing and deploying ML-AMMs requires significant expertise in both machine learning and financial markets, making these systems complex to build and maintain.

User Understanding: The complexity of ML-AMMs may make them less accessible or understandable to the average DeFi user, potentially limiting adoption.

High Computational Costs: ML models, especially deep learning algorithms, require substantial computational power and resources, which can lead to higher operational costs, particularly on blockchains with high gas fees.

Latency Issues: The need for real-time data processing and decision-making can introduce latency, which may affect the AMM's performance in fast-moving markets.

Quality of Data: The effectiveness of ML-AMMs is highly dependent on the quality and quantity of data available. Poor data quality, data sparsity, or outdated data can lead to inaccurate predictions and suboptimal decisions.

Data Privacy Concerns: Handling large amounts of sensitive financial data may raise privacy concerns, particularly in decentralized environments where data governance is less clear.

Overfitting Risk: ML models, particularly those with complex architectures, can sometimes be overfit to historical data, making them less effective in predicting future market conditions that differ from past patterns.

Generalization Challenges: Ensuring that the ML-AMM generalizes well across different market conditions is challenging and requires careful model tuning and validation.

Use Cases for ML-AMMs

Optimized Execution: ML-AMMs can optimize trading strategies in high-frequency trading scenarios, where quick, accurate decisions are crucial for minimizing slippage and maximizing profits.

Volatility Management: The ability to predict and adapt to market volatility makes ML-AMMs well-suited for high-frequency trading environments, where market conditions can change rapidly.

Structured Products: ML-AMMs can be used to create and manage structured financial products, such as options, futures, and synthetic assets, where pricing and risk management require advanced modeling and real-time adjustments.

Algorithmic Strategies: ML-AMMs can execute algorithmic trading strategies that require real-time data analysis and decision-making, providing more sophisticated trading tools for DeFi users.

Dynamic Pools: ML-AMMs can manage liquidity pools that adapt to changing market conditions, optimizing capital efficiency and ensuring that liquidity is available where it is most needed.

Risk-Aware Liquidity Management: By incorporating risk predictions, ML-AMMs can adjust liquidity provision to minimize exposure during periods of high volatility or market stress.

Tailored Strategies: ML-AMMs can offer customizable solutions for users who need specific trading or liquidity provision strategies, allowing them to optimize their DeFi participation based on personalized risk and return profiles.

DeFi Integrations: ML-AMMs can integrate with other DeFi protocols to provide more complex financial services, such as automated yield farming or dynamic asset management.

Examples of Machine Learning-Driven Automated MM

Table 9: Machine Learning Applications for DeFi Platforms

Platform	Focus	Approach	Key Parameters
VannaSwap	Reducing impermanent loss	On-chain ML models for price prediction and liquidity adjustment	Price prediction models, liquidity adjustment parameters
dYdX	Improving perpetual swap efficiency	ML algorithms for funding rate optimization	Funding rate models, price deviation parameters
Numerai	Decentralized hedge fund	Community-driven ML models	Model performance metrics, reward system
Alpha Finance Lab	DeFi products powered by ML	ML for yield farming and risk management	Yield optimization models, risk assessment parameters
Element Protocol	Decentralized options exchange	ML for option pricing	Option pricing models, risk management parameters
Cartesi	On-chain ML execution	Platform for running ML models on-chain	Model deployment and execution parameters
Chainlink Keepers	Automated tasks on-chain	ML for data analysis and action triggering	Data analysis models, action parameters
Oasis Network	Privacy-preserving DeFi	ML for data anonymization	Privacy-preserving algorithms, data anonymization techniques
Synthetix	Synthetic asset issuance	ML for pricing and management	Pricing models, risk management parameters
Paraswap	Liquidity aggregation	ML for selecting optimal AMMs	AMM selection models, price comparison parameters
dForce	DeFi products	ML for risk	Risk assessment

		management and optimization	models, optimization parameters
Reflex Finance	Decentralized options exchange	ML for option pricing	Option pricing models, risk management parameters
DeFi Pulse Index	DeFi index	ML for token selection and weighting	Token selection models, weighting algorithms
DeFi Saver	DeFi asset management	ML for automation and optimization	Automation algorithms, optimization parameters
Yearn Finance	Yield optimization	ML for identifying profitable strategies	Yield optimization models, market analysis parameters

Training Machine Learning-Driven Automated MM

Training Machine Learning-Driven Automated Market Makers (ML-AMMs) involves several steps that require a combination of financial market knowledge, data science expertise, and machine learning (ML) techniques. The goal is to develop models that can predict market behavior, optimize trading strategies, and manage risks effectively. Below is a guide on how to train ML-AMMs.

Before starting the training process, clearly define the objectives of the ML-AMM. Common objectives include:

- Price Prediction: Predict future price movements of assets.
- Volatility Prediction: Forecast market volatility to adjust trading strategies accordingly.
- Risk Management: Implement strategies to minimize risks such as impermanent loss.
- Liquidity Optimization: Optimize the allocation of liquidity in the pool to maximize capital efficiency.

Collecting high-quality data is critical for training ML models. The data should be relevant to the objectives of the ML-AMM and should include a mix of historical and real-time data.

Types of Data Needed:

Market Data: Historical price data, trading volumes, order book data, and transaction history from exchanges.
Blockchain Data: On-chain data such as wallet addresses, transaction times, and gas fees.
External Factors: Macro-economic indicators, news sentiment, social media activity, and other external factors that may influence market behavior.
Liquidity Data: Information on liquidity pools, including the amount of assets, trading fees, and impermanent loss.

Data Sources:

APIs from Exchanges: Use APIs provided by centralized and decentralized exchanges to collect market data.
Blockchain Explorers: Tools like Etherscan, BscScan, or blockchain-specific explorers can provide on-chain data.
Data Providers: Use services like Chainlink, The Graph, or Messari for aggregated and processed data.
Custom Scraping: For external factors like news or social media sentiment, web scraping or API access may be required.

Model Selection

Choosing the right machine learning model depends on the specific goals and the nature of the data. Below are some common types of models used in ML-AMMs:

Supervised Learning Models: Used for predicting specific outcomes, such as asset prices or volatility.
    Linear Regression: For simple price prediction.
    Decision Trees and Random Forests: For more complex predictions with multiple features.
    Neural Networks: For capturing non-linear relationships in the data.
Unsupervised Learning Models: Used for discovering patterns or anomalies in the data.
    Clustering Algorithms: Such as k-means, to identify similar market conditions.

Principal Component Analysis (PCA): For dimensionality reduction and identifying key market drivers.
Reinforcement Learning Models: Used for strategy optimization and decision-making in dynamic environments.
Q-Learning: For optimizing trading strategies based on reward feedback.
Deep Reinforcement Learning: For more complex environments with multiple variables and delayed rewards.
Time Series Models: Specifically designed for handling sequential data, such as price and volume history.
ARIMA: For modeling time series data and forecasting future trends.
LSTM (Long Short-Term Memory) Networks: A type of recurrent neural network (RNN) suitable for capturing temporal dependencies in time series data.

Model Training

Set the model by configuring its initial parameters, such as assigning weights in a neural network or setting decision thresholds in a decision tree. At this stage, programmer define the model's architecture and set its initial parameters. The model's parameters could be weights in a neural network or decision thresholds in a decision tree, depending on the type of model chosen.

Weights are initial guesses that the model will adjust as it learns. They are numerical values that determine how strongly a feature affects the prediction. In a neural network, the initialization also includes setting up the structure of the network, such as the number of layers and neurons in each layer.

Example for ML-AMMs:
If programmer building an ML-AMM to predict future token prices, you might initialize a neural network with two hidden layers and random initial weights for all connections between neurons. For decision trees or random forests, programmer also define the depth of the tree and decision criteria.

Feed Data to the Model: Input the training data into the model and allow it to learn the relationships between the features and the target variable (e.g., future price). In this step, the preprocessed data (features and target variables) is passed into the model. The model "learns" by processing each data point and comparing its predictions to the actual target outcomes (e.g., actual asset prices). Features are the input variables, like historical price data, volume, or market indicators, while the target could be a future asset price or volatility level. The model looks at these relationships and updates its internal parameters based on the patterns it identifies.

For example, if the goal is to predict future prices, programmer might input historical price data of tokens, and the target variable would be the actual price a few hours or days later. The model will try to predict future prices based on past patterns and adjust itself according to the accuracy of its predictions. Utilizing optimization algorithms, such as gradient descent, to reduce the discrepancy between predicted and actual outcomes.

After the model makes predictions, it measures how far off these predictions are from the actual outcomes (called the error or loss). The model then adjusts its parameters (like weights) to reduce this error. The process of updating these parameters is called "optimization", and the most common technique used is gradient descent[31]. Gradient descent iteratively adjusts the model's parameters to minimize the difference between predicted and actual values. This process repeats for multiple epochs[32] (training iterations), allowing the model to gradually improve its accuracy.

Example for ML-AMMs:

Suppose your ML-AMM is predicting a token price. After each prediction, it calculates how far off the prediction is compared to the actual price. Using gradient descent, it adjusts the model weights (parameters) so that future predictions get closer to the actual price.

Validation: Regularly validate the model using the validation dataset to ensure it is not overfitting to the training data. Adjust hyperparameters (e.g., learning rate, number of layers) based on validation performance.

Validation ensures the model is not only learning patterns in the training data but also generalizing well to new, unseen data. During training, you set aside a portion of the data (called the validation set) that the model does not see during training. The model is tested on this validation set

---

[31] https://www.ibm.com/topics/gradient-descent
[32] https://deepai.org/machine-learning-glossary-and-terms/epoch

after each training epoch. If the model performs well on both the training and validation sets, it means it is learning useful patterns. However, if it performs well on the training data but poorly on the validation set, it's likely overfitting (memorizing the training data without generalizing).

During validation, programmer might adjust hyperparameters, which are settings like the learning rate (how quickly the model learns), the number of layers, or the batch[33] size. Iterative Improvement: Iterate the training process multiple times, refining the model each time to improve its accuracy and robustness.

Example for ML-AMMs:
As programmer train its ML-AMM to predict token prices, programmer periodically evaluate it on the validation set (data the model hasn't seen). If the model is overfitting[34], you might reduce the number of layers (Layers in a neural network are collections of interconnected nodes which are such as neurons that process input data and pass the output to subsequent layers, enabling feature extraction and decision-making) in the neural network or slow down the learning rate to prevent it from memorizing the training data.

<u>Iterative Improvement:</u> Training is an iterative process, where the model undergoes multiple cycles (epochs) of learning, adjusting, and validation. After each cycle, the model is refined based on the feedback from the validation set and the optimization process. If necessary, programmer can fine-tune the hyperparameters (like the learning rate, number of epochs, or network structure) to improve performance. With each iteration, the model learns to make more accurate predictions or decisions.

Example for ML-AMMs:
Let's say a ML-AMM initially makes poor price predictions. After a few iterations, programmer observe that lowering the learning rate improves accuracy. Programmer might also add more training data or adjust the depth of your neural network until the model consistently makes reliable predictions.

---

[33] https://machinelearningmastery.com/difference-between-a-batch-and-an-epoch/
[34] https://www.ibm.com/topics/overfitting

Evaluation and Testing

After training, the model should be rigorously evaluated using the test dataset to ensure it performs well on unseen data.

Evaluation Metrics:

Mean Squared Error (MSE): Measures the average squared difference between predicted and actual values, commonly used for regression tasks.
Accuracy: The percentage of correct predictions, useful for classification tasks.
Precision, Recall, "F1-Score" (a machine learning evaluation metric that measures a model's accuracy): For evaluating models in scenarios where false positives or false negatives are important.
Sharpe Ratio (which measures the risk-adjusted return of an investment by comparing its excess return (over a risk-free rate) to its standard deviation of returns): Measures the risk-adjusted return, useful for evaluating ai based and other financial models.
Confusion Matrix: For analyzing the performance of classification models.

Testing Scenarios:

Backtesting: Simulate the model's performance using historical data to assess how well it would have performed in real market conditions.
Stress Testing: Evaluate the model's robustness under extreme market conditions (e.g., market crashes, high volatility periods).
Live Testing: Deploy the model in a live environment with limited capital to test its performance in real-time market conditions.

Deployment

Once the model is trained and tested, it can be deployed as part of the AMM's smart contract or as an external service that interacts with the AMM.

Deployment Steps:

Smart Contract Integration: If the ML model is to be embedded directly into the AMM, it must be converted into a format compatible with smart contracts (e.g., Solidity for Ethereum).

API Deployment: The model can also be deployed as a service, interacting with the AMM via APIs to provide real-time predictions or trading signals.

Monitoring and Maintenance: Continuously monitor the model's performance post-deployment. Regularly retrain the model with new data to adapt to changing market conditions.

Continuous Learning and Improvement

Markets are dynamic, and ML-AMMs must adapt to new data and evolving conditions.

Regular Retraining: Periodically retrain the model using the latest data to ensure it remains accurate and effective.

Feedback Loops: Incorporate feedback from the model's live performance to fine-tune its parameters and improve its predictions.

Model Updating: Experiment with new algorithms or model architectures to keep up with advances in machine learning and adapt to the changing financial landscape.

Figure 1: Types of Models in Machine Learning

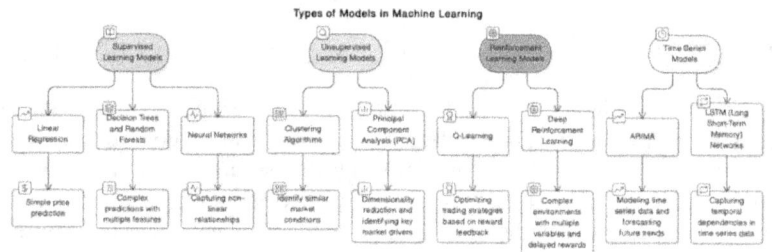

Objectives for Machine Learning-Driven Automated MM

Before starting the training process for a Machine Learning-Driven Automated Market Maker (ML-AMM), it is key to clearly define the specific objectives the ML model aims to achieve. These objectives guide the choice of data, model architecture, and evaluation metrics. The objectives are directly related to the primary goals of the AMM, such as optimizing trading strategies, managing risks, and enhancing liquidity provision. Here, we detail some common objectives for ML-AMMs:

Price Prediction

Goal: Predict future price movements of assets traded within the AMM. Accurate price predictions allow the AMM to set more competitive prices, minimize slippage, and improve the overall trading experience.

In decentralized exchanges (DEXs) powered by AMMs, prices are often determined algorithmically based on the ratio of assets in a liquidity pool. However, these prices might not always align with broader market prices, especially in volatile conditions or when liquidity is low. ML models can help align AMM prices more closely with market trends, reducing arbitrage opportunities and improving user satisfaction.

Data Requirements: Historical price data, order book data (from centralized exchanges for comparison), trading volumes, market news, social media sentiment, and macroeconomic indicators.

Model Types: Time series models like ARIMA, Long Short-Term Memory (LSTM) networks, or deep learning models like convolutional neural networks (CNNs) for complex pattern recognition.

Evaluation Metrics: Mean Squared Error (MSE), Mean Absolute Error (MAE), and accuracy in predicting price direction (up or down).

Market Noise: Financial markets are inherently noisy, and distinguishing between meaningful trends and random fluctuations can be challenging.

Overfitting: There is a risk that the model may be overfit to historical data, reducing its ability to generalize to future market conditions.

Volatility Prediction

Forecast future market volatility to adjust trading strategies and liquidity provision accordingly. Volatility prediction helps in optimizing the AMM's parameters, such as trading fees, slippage tolerance, and liquidity allocation.

Importance: Volatility is a critical factor in financial markets, affecting pricing, liquidity, and the risk associated with holding or trading assets. By predicting periods of high volatility, the AMM can proactively adjust its operations to manage risks and maintain stability in the liquidity pool.

Data Requirements: Historical volatility measures (e.g., standard deviation of returns, implied volatility from options), market sentiment data, economic indicators, and recent price movements.

Model Types:
Generalized Autoregressive Conditional Heteroskedasticity (GARCH) models, LSTM networks, or reinforcement learning models for adaptive volatility management.

Evaluation Metrics: Forecast accuracy (e.g., Root Mean Squared Error - RMSE), ability to predict spikes in volatility, and the model's impact on reducing volatility-related risks (e.g., reducing slippage during high volatility periods).

Sudden Market Shifts: Volatility can spike unexpectedly due to unforeseen events (e.g., economic news, regulatory changes), making prediction difficult.

Data Sensitivity: Volatility models are highly sensitive to the quality and timeliness of the data, requiring constant updates and recalibration.

Risk Management

Implement strategies to minimize financial risks associated with operating an AMM, such as impermanent loss, market exposure, and liquidity depletion. Effective risk management ensures that liquidity providers (LPs) are protected from potential losses, making the AMM more attractive for users.

Impermanent loss, a unique risk in AMMs, occurs when the price of assets in a liquidity pool diverges from the price at which they were deposited. Managing this and other risks is essential for maintaining the financial health of the AMM and retaining LPs.

Data Requirements: Asset price data, historical performance of liquidity pools, market conditions, trading volume trends, and user behavior analytics.

Model Types: Reinforcement learning models that learn to balance risk and return over time, decision trees for implementing risk thresholds, or Bayesian networks for probabilistic risk assessment.

Evaluation Metrics: Reduction in impermanent loss, improved stability of the liquidity pool, and overall return on investment (ROI) for liquidity providers.

Balancing Trade-offs: Effective risk management often involves trade-offs, such as balancing the desire for high returns with the need to minimize risk, which must be carefully managed.

Liquidity Optimization

Optimize the allocation of liquidity within the AMM to maximize capital efficiency and minimize slippage. This involves ensuring that sufficient liquidity is available where it is most needed, without overcommitting resources that could be used more effectively elsewhere. Without sufficient liquidity, trades can suffer from high slippage, making the platform less attractive to users. Conversely, excessive liquidity in a low-volume pool can lead to inefficiencies, tying up capital that could be better used in other pools.

Optimization algorithms, such as linear programming, or machine learning models like reinforcement learning, which can dynamically adjust liquidity allocations based on real-time market data. Reduction in slippage, improvement in trading volume, and enhanced returns for liquidity providers through more efficient capital use.

Market conditions can change rapidly, requiring the model to continuously adapt and re-optimize liquidity allocations. Implementing dynamic liquidity adjustments in a decentralized environment requires careful coordination between the ML model and the underlying blockchain infrastructure.

As of 2024, the DeFi market is poised for significant growth, with a market size projected to reach $78.47 billion by 2029, growing at a compound annual growth rate (CAGR) of 10.98%. Within this expansive market, AMMs are a core technology, facilitating billions of dollars in daily trading volume. AMMs like Uniswap, SushiSwap, and Balancer have become household names in the DeFi space, each handling significant portions of the total value locked (TVL) across DeFi protocols.

Decentralized Exchanges (DEXs)

DEXs allow users to trade cryptocurrencies directly with one another without relying on an intermediary, like a centralized exchange.

- Example: Uniswap is a DEX that uses liquidity pools to facilitate trading without a central order book.

Decentralized Exchanges (DEXs) have emerged as pivotal components of the decentralized finance (DeFi) ecosystem, offering an alternative to traditional centralized exchanges (CEXs). Unlike their centralized counterparts, DEXs operate without intermediaries, enabling peer-to-peer (P2P) trading of cryptocurrencies directly between users. This detailed explanation explores the fundamental aspects of DEXs, their operational mechanisms, advantages and disadvantages, and prominent examples in the market.

DEXs are platforms that facilitate the trading of cryptocurrencies without relying on a central authority or intermediary. Instead, they leverage blockchain technology and smart contracts to enable users to retain control of their funds throughout the trading process.

Key Characteristics of DEXs:

Non-Custodial: Users retain ownership of their private keys and funds, reducing the risk of hacks associated with centralized storage.

Trustless Environment: Trades are executed via smart contracts, eliminating the need to trust a central entity.

Permissionless: Typically, open to anyone with an internet connection and a compatible wallet, without requiring extensive verification processes.

Transparent: All transactions are recorded on the blockchain, ensuring transparency and immutability.

How Do DEXs Work?

DEXs operate on blockchain networks, primarily Ethereum, Binance Smart Chain (BSC), and others like Solana and Polygon. They utilize smart contracts to facilitate and automate the trading process. There are two primary models for DEX operations:

Order Book-Based DEXs

Order Book-Based DEXs mimic the traditional trading system found in centralized exchanges. They maintain an order book where buy and sell orders are listed, and matching algorithms execute trades when compatible orders are found.

Order Placement: Traders place limit or market orders specifying the amount and price of the asset they wish to buy or sell.

Order Matching: The DEX's matching engine pairs compatible buy and sell orders.

Trade Execution: Once matched, the smart contracts facilitate the transfer of assets between parties.

Examples:

> dYdX: A prominent decentralized exchange offering advanced trading features like margin trading and perpetual contracts.
>
> Loopring: Utilizes zkRollup[35] technology to enhance scalability and reduce transaction costs.

Advantages:

> Familiar Interface: Resembles traditional exchanges, making it easier for users transitioning from CEXs.
>
> Advanced Trading Features: Supports complex order types and trading strategies.

---

[35] https://chain.link/education-hub/zero-knowledge-rollup

Disadvantages:

> Liquidity Challenges: May suffer from lower liquidity compared to AMM-based DEXs.
>
> Higher Gas Fees: Especially on networks like Ethereum, leading to increased transaction costs.

Automated Market Maker (AMM)-Based DEXs

AMM-Based DEXs use liquidity pools and mathematical formulas to determine asset prices, eliminating the need for order books.

How They Work:

Liquidity Pools: Users (liquidity providers or LPs) deposit pairs of tokens into pools.

Pricing Formula: A predefined algorithm (e.g., Constant Product Market Maker) sets the price based on the ratio of assets in the pool.

Swapping: Traders swap tokens directly from the pool, with prices adjusting automatically based on the trade size and pool ratios.

Examples:

Uniswap: One of the first and most widely used AMM-based DEXs, operating on Ethereum.

SushiSwap: A Uniswap fork that introduced additional features like yield farming and staking.

PancakeSwap: Operates on BSC, offering lower transaction fees and a variety of DeFi features.

Advantages:

> Enhanced Liquidity: Often benefits from larger liquidity pools, reducing slippage.
>
> Simplified Trading: Users can trade directly from their wallets without the need for order matching.

Incentives for Liquidity Providers: LPs earn fees from trades, incentivizing them to provide liquidity.

Disadvantages:

Impermanent Loss: LPs may experience losses due to price fluctuations of the pooled assets.

Price Slippage: Large trades can significantly alter pool ratios, leading to slippage.

Advantages of Decentralized Exchanges

Self-Custody: Users retain control over their funds, mitigating risks associated with exchange hacks or mismanagement.

Reduced Counterparty Risk: No reliance on a central authority ensures that funds are not susceptible to centralized failures.

Minimal KYC Requirements: Most DEXs do not require extensive identity verification, preserving user privacy.

Pseudonymous Transactions: Users can trade without revealing their real-world identities.

Global Access: Available to anyone with internet access, irrespective of geographical location.

On-Chain Transactions: All trades and liquidity pools are transparent and auditable on the blockchain.

Smart Contract Audits: Open-source code allows for community audits and verification.

Disadvantages of Decentralized Exchanges

Complexity: Navigating wallets, understanding gas fees, and interacting with smart contracts can be overwhelming for beginners.

Interface Limitations: Some DEXs may lack the advanced features and intuitive interfaces found in CEXs.

Fragmented Liquidity: Liquidity may be spread across multiple DEXs, making it challenging to find the best prices.

Smaller Liquidity Pools: Compared to major CEXs, some DEXs may have limited liquidity, affecting trade execution.

High Gas Fees: Particularly on Ethereum, gas fees can become prohibitively expensive during network congestion.

Slower Transactions: Confirmation times can vary based on network conditions, affecting trade speed.

Fewer Listings: While growing, the number of listed assets on DEXs may be fewer compared to CEXs.

Smart Contract Risks: Vulnerabilities in smart contracts can lead to exploits or loss of funds.

Examples of Decentralized Exchanges

Uniswap

Launched in 2018 on the Ethereum blockchain, Uniswap popularized the Automated Market Maker (AMM) model, enabling trustless token swaps without an order book. Key Features: Liquidity Pools allow users to provide liquidity by depositing pairs of ERC-20 tokens. The UNI Token is a governance token that allows holders to participate in protocol decisions. Version 3 Innovations introduced concentrated liquidity, enabling liquidity providers to allocate liquidity within specific price ranges for increased capital efficiency. Use Case Example: A user can swap ETH for DAI directly from their wallet by interacting with the Uniswap smart contract, receiving the best available rate based on the current pool ratio.

SushiSwap

Launched in 2020 as a Uniswap fork, SushiSwap introduced additional features like yield farming and governance through its SUSHI token. Key Features: Yield Farming allows LPs to stake their liquidity pool tokens to earn additional rewards. The SUSHI Token grants governance rights and rewards holders with a portion of the trading fees. Multi-

Chain Support enables the platform to operate on multiple blockchains beyond Ethereum, such as Binance Smart Chain (BSC) and Polygon. Use Case Example: A liquidity provider can deposit ETH and USDT into a SushiSwap pool, earn trading fees, and stake their liquidity tokens to receive SUSHI rewards.

PancakeSwap

Operating on the Binance Smart Chain (BSC), PancakeSwap offers similar functionalities to Uniswap but with lower transaction fees and faster confirmations. Key Features: The CAKE Token is the native governance and utility token used for staking and lotteries. Yield Farms and Syrup Pools allow users to stake CAKE or other tokens to earn rewards. The NFT Marketplace offers unique non-fungible tokens for users to collect and trade. Use Case Example: Traders can swap BEP-20 tokens like BNB and CAKE with minimal gas fees, participate in lotteries using CAKE tokens, and stake their tokens in yield farms to earn additional rewards.

Curve Finance

Specialized in stablecoin trading, Curve Finance utilizes a unique Automated Market Maker (AMM) designed to offer low slippage and minimal fees for assets with similar values. Key Features: Stablecoin Pools are optimized for swapping between stablecoins like USDC, USDT, and DAI. The CRV Token serves as a governance and utility token, enabling voting on protocol upgrades and fee distributions. Integration with Other DeFi Protocols supports liquidity provision to other platforms, enhancing capital efficiency. Use Case Example: A user can efficiently swap between USDC and DAI with minimal slippage and fees, making Curve ideal for stablecoin arbitrage and liquidity provision.

Balancer

Balancer extends the Automated Market Maker (AMM) concept by allowing multi-asset pools with customizable weightings, acting as both an exchange and a portfolio manager. Key Features: Customizable Pools enable pools to contain multiple tokens with varying weights, facilitating complex trading strategies. The BAL Token is a governance token that rewards users for participating in the network. Smart Pool Technology allows for dynamic fee structures and automated portfolio rebalancing. Use Case Example: An investor can create a Balancer pool with ETH, DAI, and USDC in a 60:30:10 ratio, earning trading fees from users swapping within the pool while maintaining a diversified asset portfolio.

Comparing DEXs with Centralized Exchanges (CEXs)

Table 10: Comparison of DEXs and CEXs

Aspect	Decentralized Exchanges (DEXs)	Centralized Exchanges (CEXs)
Control of Funds	Users retain custody of their funds	Exchanges hold and manage user funds
Security	Reduced risk of exchange hacks; depends on smart contract security	Higher risk of large-scale hacks due to centralized fund storage
Privacy	Enhanced privacy; minimal to no KYC requirements	Requires extensive KYC/AML procedures
Liquidity	Often fragmented across multiple DEXs.	Generally higher and more concentrated liquidity
User Experience	Can be complex; requires understanding of wallets and gas fees	User-friendly interfaces; familiar to traditional traders
Asset Availability	Limited to tokens listed on the specific DEX	Wider range of listed assets, including fiat gateways and derivatives
Fees	Depends on network fees	trading fees, withdrawal fees, and other hidden costs
Regulation	Largely unregulated; operates in a decentralized manner	Subject to strict regulatory oversight and compliance requirements
Transaction Speed	Dependent on blockchain network congestion	Generally faster and more consistent

The Future of Decentralized Exchanges

DEXs continue to evolve, addressing current limitations and expanding their functionalities. Key trends and future directions include:

Cross-Chain Compatibility enhances interoperability between different blockchain networks to facilitate seamless asset transfers and trading. Layer 2 Solutions involve implementing scalability solutions like rollups to reduce transaction costs and increase throughput. Enhanced User Interfaces focus on developing more intuitive and user-friendly interfaces to attract mainstream users. Integration with Traditional Finance bridges the gap between DeFi and traditional financial systems through hybrid models and regulated offerings. Advanced Financial Instruments introduce features like options, futures, and synthetic assets to provide more sophisticated trading options.

Cross-Chain Compatibility in DeFi

Cross-chain compatibility refers to the ability of different blockchain networks to interact with each other seamlessly, enabling the transfer of assets, data, and value across disparate blockchain platforms. In the context of DeFi, cross-chain compatibility is crucial for enhancing interoperability, which allows users to leverage the unique features of various blockchains without being confined to a single network.

Cross-chain compatibility is vital in decentralized finance (DeFi) for several reasons:

Expanding Market Access: Cross-chain compatibility allows users to access a broader range of assets and services across multiple blockchain networks. For example, a user on the Ethereum network can seamlessly interact with assets and DeFi protocols on Binance Smart Chain (BSC), Solana, or Polkadot, thereby expanding their investment and diversified opportunities. This accessibility also increases the overall liquidity available in the DeFi ecosystem, leading to more efficient markets, better price discovery.

Mitigating Blockchain Limitations: Different blockchains offer varying levels of scalability and performance. Ethereum, known for its robust

DeFi ecosystem, often suffers from high gas fees and network congestion. Cross-chain solutions allow users to leverage the high throughput and low fees of alternative blockchains like Solana or Binance Smart Chain while still accessing Ethereum's DeFi services. Additionally, cross-chain compatibility enables users to choose blockchains based on their preferred security and decentralization levels, such as storing assets on a highly secure and decentralized network like Bitcoin while using them in DeFi applications on Ethereum.

Enabling Complex DeFi Strategies: Cross-chain compatibility facilitates complex DeFi strategies such as cross-chain arbitrage, where traders can exploit price differences for the same asset on different blockchains. It also enables the creation of interoperable financial products, such as decentralized derivatives or synthetic assets that draw value from multiple blockchain networks. These products provide more diverse and sophisticated investment opportunities for users, enhancing the overall functionality and appeal of DeFi.

Mechanisms for Achieving Cross-Chain Compatibility

Cross-Chain Bridges: Cross-chain bridges are protocols that enable the transfer of assets between different blockchain networks. They typically work by locking an asset on the source chain and minting an equivalent token on the destination chain. When the user wants to transfer the asset back, the token on the destination chain is burned, and the original asset is released on the source chain. For example, RenBridge (Ren36 is an open protocol that enables the movement of value between blockchains) is a cross-chain bridge that allows users to transfer assets like Bitcoin, Bitcoin Cash, and Zcash to Ethereum, where they can be used in Ethereum-based DeFi applications.

Wrapped Tokens: Wrapped tokens are representations of an asset from one blockchain on another blockchain. For instance, Wrapped Bitcoin (WBTC) is a token on the Ethereum network that represents Bitcoin. It is backed 1:1 by Bitcoin held in reserve by a custodian. Wrapped tokens

---

[36] https://polygon.technology/blog/bridge-your-assets-through-renbridge-on-polygon

enable the use of non-native assets on a different blockchain while maintaining their value. An example is Wrapped Bitcoin (WBTC), which allows Bitcoin holders to use their BTC in Ethereum-based DeFi protocols like Uniswap, Aave, or Compound.

Interoperability Protocols: Interoperability protocols are designed to connect multiple blockchains, allowing them to communicate and share data directly. These protocols typically involve more complex mechanisms than simple asset transfer, enabling the execution of smart contracts across different blockchains. An example is Polkadot[37], an interoperability protocol that allows different blockchains (parachains[38]) to interoperate through its central relay chain. This setup enables cross-chain communication, asset transfers, and the execution of cross-chain smart contracts.

Atomic Swaps: Atomic swaps[39] enable the direct exchange of one cryptocurrency for another between different blockchains without the need for an intermediary. This is achieved using smart contracts that enforce the swap only if both parties fulfill their obligations, ensuring that the exchange is trustless and secure. An atomic swap could allow a user to exchange Bitcoin for Ethereum directly from their wallets without using a centralized exchange or bridge.

Cross-chain DEXs are trading platforms that facilitate the exchange of assets across different blockchains by utilizing cross-chain bridges or interoperability protocols. They allow users to trade tokens from one blockchain for tokens on another seamlessly. An example is ThorChain[40], a cross-chain DEX that enables users to swap native assets across different blockchains like Bitcoin, Ethereum, and Binance Smart Chain without wrapping tokens or relying on centralized intermediaries.

Challenges in Cross-Chain Compatibility

Security Risks: Vulnerabilities in bridges are a major concern as these are often targets for attacks due to the significant amounts of assets

---

[37] https://polkadot.com
[38] https://polkadot.com/parachains
[39] https://chain.link/education-hub/atomic-swaps
[40] https://thorchain.org/swap

locked in smart contracts. A compromised bridge can lead to substantial losses. Additionally, the complexity involved in creating interoperability protocols that enable seamless interaction between different blockchains can introduce vulnerabilities that are difficult to detect and mitigate.

Scalability Issues: Cross-chain compatibility can lead to increased transaction volumes on multiple networks, which may exacerbate scalability issues, particularly on blockchains already facing congestion. Managing cross-chain transactions can also be resource-intensive, requiring more computational power, storage, and bandwidth, which can increase operational costs and latency.

Consensus and Governance: Achieving consensus across multiple blockchains is challenging, especially when these blockchains use different consensus mechanisms, such as "Proof of Work" versus "Proof of Stake". Coordinating these mechanisms can be complex and requires careful design to avoid conflicts or delays. Additionally, when assets or data are transferred across chains, the governance frameworks of the involved blockchains can conflict, necessitating careful attention to ensure that the rules of one blockchain do not violate the principles of another.

User Experience: The process of moving assets across chains can be complex and intimidating for users, particularly those who are less experienced with blockchain technology. Simplifying the user experience while maintaining security is a significant challenge. Moreover, cross-chain transactions can involve multiple fees, including gas fees on both the source and destination chains, bridge fees, and possible slippage. These costs can add up, making cross-chain transactions less attractive to users.

Examples of Cross-Chain Projects in DeFi

Polkadot and Parachains: "Polkadot" is designed to facilitate cross-chain compatibility by allowing multiple blockchains to connect to its central relay chain. This setup enables the seamless transfer of assets and data between different "parachains", promoting interoperability across the Polkadot ecosystem. A DeFi protocol on one "parachain" can access assets or services on another one without requiring users to switch networks or manage multiple wallets.

ThorChain: This is a decentralized liquidity protocol that enables cross-chain swaps without wrapping assets. It uses its native token, "RUNE", to facilitate the exchange of assets like Bitcoin, Ethereum, and Binance Coin across their respective blockchains. A user can swap Bitcoin directly for Ethereum on ThorChain, without needing to convert Bitcoin to Wrapped Bitcoin (WBTC) first, ensuring the trade remains fully decentralized.

Cosmos and the Inter-Blockchain Communication Protocol[41] (IBC): Cosmos is an interoperability protocol that uses IBC protocol to enable different blockchains within the Cosmos network to communicate and transfer assets seamlessly. A DeFi application on one Cosmos chain (e.g., Terra) can interact with another chain (e.g., Osmosis) to offer users cross-chain yield farming opportunities.

RenVM (Ren Protocol[42]): RenVM is a protocol that facilitates the transfer of assets like Bitcoin, Zcash, and Bitcoin Cash to Ethereum, where they can be used in Ethereum-based DeFi protocols. It operates as a decentralized custodian, locking assets on their native chains and minting equivalent tokens on Ethereum. A user can lock Bitcoin in RenVM and receive renBTC, which can then be used as "collateral in Ethereum" based DeFi protocols like Aave or Compound.

The future of DeFi is likely to be multi-chain, with users and protocols interacting across a diverse array of blockchain networks. Cross-chain compatibility will play a pivotal role in this evolution by creating a unified DeFi ecosystem where users can freely move assets and data, access decentralized applications (dApps), and leverage financial services across multiple networks. As cross-chain technology matures, it will enable the creation of more sophisticated and interoperable financial products that draw on the strengths of various blockchain platforms. Innovations in cross-chain technology will also improve the user experience, making it easier for users to navigate a multi-chain DeFi

---

[41] https://www.ibcprotocol.dev
[42] https://renprotocol.org

landscape without having to manage multiple wallets, bridges, or complex transactions.

Layer 2 Solutions in DeFi DEXs

Layer 2 (L2) solutions are protocols built on top of an existing blockchain (Layer 1, such as Ethereum) to enhance its scalability, reduce transaction costs, and increase throughput without compromising security or decentralization. In the context of Decentralized Exchanges (DEXs) within the DeFi ecosystem, Layer 2 solutions are critical for addressing the challenges associated with high transaction fees and network congestion, particularly on popular Layer 1 blockchains like Ethereum.

Why Layer 2 Solutions are Important for DEXs in DeFi:

Scalability Issues on Layer 1: High Gas Fees: On Layer 1 blockchains like Ethereum, each transaction requires a fee (gas) paid to miners. During periods of high network activity, these fees can skyrocket, making small or frequent trades prohibitively expensive for users. Network Congestion: High demand for block space on Layer 1 can result in slow transaction times, creating challenges for DEX users who need fast and efficient trading to capitalize on market opportunities.

Need for Enhanced User Experience: By reducing transaction costs, Layer 2 solutions make DeFi more accessible to a broader audience, including retail traders who may be priced out of the market by high fees. Increased throughput and reduced latency on Layer 2 improve the overall user experience, enabling faster order execution and settlement on DEXs.

Maintaining Security and Decentralization: Layer 2 solutions inherit the security properties of the underlying Layer 1 blockchain, ensuring that transactions are secure and tamper-proof while providing the benefits of increased scalability and lower costs. Unlike centralized solutions, Layer 2 maintains the decentralized nature of DeFi, ensuring that users retain control over their assets without relying on a central authority.

Types of Layer 2 Solutions for DeFi DEXs

Rollups: Overview: Rollups are one of the most popular Layer 2 scaling solutions. They work by bundling (or "rolling up") multiple transactions into a single batch, which is then submitted to the Layer 1 blockchain. Rollups handle most of the transaction processing off-chain, while only minimal data is posted on-chain, reducing the load on the main blockchain.

Types of Rollups: "Optimistic Rollups" assume that transactions are valid by default and only execute a fraud-proof mechanism if a dispute arises. This makes them more efficient but with a slight delay in finality due to the challenge period. ZK-Rollups (Zero-Knowledge Rollups): Use cryptographic proofs (zero-knowledge proofs) to ensure the validity of transactions off-chain, with immediate finality and no need for a challenge period. Example: Arbitrum (an Optimistic Rollup) and zkSync (a ZK-Rollup) are two prominent Layer 2 solutions that DEXs can integrate to enhance scalability.

Also, "State channels[43]" allow multiple transactions between parties to be conducted off-chain, with only the final state being recorded on the Layer 1 blockchain. This reduces the number of on-chain transactions, thus lowering fees and increasing speed.

Use Case: "State channels" are well-suited for scenarios involving frequent transactions between a small number of participants, such as micro-trades in a DEX.

Other concept is "Plasma Cahins[44]" which is a framework for creating scalable applications by running them on sub-chains connected to the main Ethereum chain. These sub-chains can process transactions independently, reducing the load on the main chain. "Plasma chain" is suitable for applications requiring high throughput and is used to move complex computations off-chain while periodically committing the results to the main chain.

---

[43] https://www.ledger.com/academy/glossary/state-channels
[44] https://ethereum.org/en/developers/docs/scaling/plasma

"Sidechains" are independent blockchains that run parallel to the main blockchain (Layer 1) but are connected to it via a two-way bridge[45]. Sidechains can handle many transactions independently and then batch settle on the main chain. Example: Polygon is a popular sidechain solution that is often used by DEXs to provide faster and cheaper transactions while still being connected to Ethereum.

How Layer 2 Solutions Enhance DEX Performance

Reducing Transaction Costs: By processing most transactions off-chain, Layer 2 solutions significantly reduce the gas fees associated with each trade. For example, a trade on a Layer 2 DEX using a rollup could cost a fraction of what it would on Layer 1. This cost efficiency makes small trades viable, allowing users to engage in high-frequency trading without being penalized by high fees.

Increasing Transaction Throughput with "Batch" Processing: Rollups and other Layer 2 solutions process multiple transactions in a batch before submitting them to the Layer 1 chain, drastically increasing the number of transactions that can be processed per second. Faster Settlements: State channels and rollups enable near-instant transaction settlements, providing a more responsive trading experience compared to the delays sometimes experienced on Layer 1.

Enhancing User Experience: With Layer 2, transactions are confirmed almost immediately, which is critical for traders who need to execute orders quickly in volatile markets. Also, Layer 2 solutions provide the scalability needed for DEXs to support a growing number of users and trades without sacrificing performance.

Maintaining Security and Decentralization: Despite operating off-chain, Layer 2 solutions inherit the security of the underlying Layer 1 blockchain. This ensures that the transactions processed on Layer 2 are as secure as those on the main chain. Layer 2 maintains the decentralized nature of DEXs, ensuring that users do not have to rely on centralized intermediaries for transaction processing.

---

[45] https://ethereum.org/en/developers/docs/scaling/sidechains

Examples of DEXs Using Layer 2 Solutions

Uniswap V3 on Optimism: Uniswap V3 integrates with Optimism to provide a Layer 2 scaling solution, allowing users to trade with lower fees and faster transaction times compared to Layer 1 Ethereum. Users can execute trades quickly and cheaply, making Uniswap V3 on Optimism particularly attractive for smaller traders who are priced out by high Layer 1 gas fees.

Loopring[46]: Layer 2 Solution: "zkRollups": Loopring is a DEX built on ZK-Rollups, allowing for high-speed, low-cost trading on Ethereum. Loopring batches thousands of trades into a single transaction that is settled on the Ethereum main network. Loopring users benefit from reduced gas fees, faster trade execution, and the security guarantees of Ethereum, making it efficient DEXs in the DeFi.

dYdX: Layer 2 Solution: StarkWare[47] (a ZK-Rollup): dYdX uses StarkWare's ZK-Rollup technology to offer perpetual trading with zero gas fees and instant trade finality on Layer 2. Traders on dYdX can experience the benefits of high-frequency trading with minimal fees and without compromising on security, because of the ZK-Rollup architecture.

Synthetix on Optimism: Layer 2 Solution: Synthetix, a protocol for trading synthetic assets, has integrated with Optimism[48] to reduce the cost and improve the speed of transactions for minting and trading synthetic assets. Users can trade synthetic assets (Synthetic assets in crypto are tokenized derivatives that replicate the value of real-world assets, such as stocks or commodities, enabling decentralized trading and investment) like sUSD, sBTC, and sETH with reduced transaction costs and faster execution, enhancing the overall experience on the Synthetix platform.

---

[46] https://loopring.org/#/
[47] https://starkware.co
[48] https://www.coinbase.com/learn/wallet/what-is-optimism

Challenges and Considerations

Technical Challenges: Integrating Layer 2 solutions with existing DEXs requires significant technical expertise, particularly when ensuring seamless interoperability between Layer 1 and Layer 2. The shift to Layer 2 may require users to understand new concepts (e.g., bridging assets to Layer 2), which can be a barrier to adoption.

Liquidity Distribution: Moving to Layer 2 can fragment liquidity across different layers, potentially leading to thinner markets on Layer 1 and reduced liquidity on Layer 2. Cross-Layer Arbitrage: Traders might need to engage in cross-layer arbitrage to balance prices, which could introduce additional complexity and costs.

Fraud Proofs and Challenges: Optimistic Rollups rely on a fraud-proof mechanism where malicious transactions can be challenged. However, this challenge process introduces a delay in finalizing transactions, which could affect the user experience. Layer 2 solutions involve complex smart contracts, which could introduce new vulnerabilities and risks if not properly audited and tested.

Centralization Concerns: Some Layer 2 solutions, especially early implementations, might rely on more centralized entities for validation and transaction processing, which could undermine the decentralized ethos of DeFi.

Broader Adoption: More DEXs are likely to integrate Layer 2 solutions, making DeFi more accessible and reducing the reliance on Layer 1 chains, particularly during periods of high congestion. Advances in Layer 2 technology, such as seamless bridging and better wallet support, will enhance the user experience, making it easier for users to interact with DeFi on Layer 2. As multiple Layer 2 solutions are developed, ensuring interoperability between them will be crucial for maintaining liquidity and enabling smooth cross-layer transactions.

Enhanced User Interfaces (UIs) in DeFi DEXs

As Decentralized Exchanges continue to gain traction in the DeFi ecosystem, one of the critical factors determining their success and mainstream adoption is the quality of their user interfaces (UIs). Unlike traditional centralized exchanges, which often provide to users who may not be deeply familiar with blockchain technology, DEXs must overcome additional challenges such as the complexity of decentralized systems and the learning curve associated with managing digital assets. Enhanced UIs play a pivotal role in making these platforms more accessible, user-friendly, and attractive to broader investors.

Importance of Enhanced User Interfaces in DeFi DEXs

Lowering the Barrier to Entry: DeFi can be intimidating for newcomers due to its technical jargon, the need to manage private keys, and the process of interacting with smart contracts. An enhanced UI can abstract these complexities, making it easier for users to engage with DeFi services without needing deep technical knowledge. By providing an interface that feels familiar to users of traditional financial services, DEXs can attract non-crypto individuals, thereby expanding their user base.

Improving User Experience (UX): A well-designed UI ensures that users can navigate the platform intuitively, finding the services they need (e.g., swapping tokens, providing liquidity, staking) without confusion. Enhanced UIs offer clear visual feedback and guidance throughout the transaction process, helping users avoid mistakes and understand the consequences of their actions.

Increasing Trust and Confidence: A transparent and well-explained interface increases user confidence by clearly showing transaction details, potential fees, and the steps involved in using the platform. This is crucial in a decentralized environment where users are responsible for their funds. Enhanced UIs can incorporate security prompts and warnings that alert users to potential risks, such as high slippage, network congestion, or unverified tokens, thereby reducing the likelihood of user errors or scams.

Personalized User Experience: UIs that adapt to individual user preferences, such as saving frequent trading pairs or customizing dashboards, can make the platform more engaging and increase user retention. Integrating "gamification" elements, such as achievements, rewards, and leaderboards, can make the platform more interactive and fun, encouraging users to return regularly.

Key Features of Enhanced UIs in DeFi DEXs

Interactive Tutorials: Provide step-by-step guides and interactive tutorials that walk users through the process of connecting a wallet, making a trade, or providing liquidity. These tutorials can be embedded directly into the UI, offering real-time assistance. Incorporate educational content, such as FAQs, glossaries, and explainer videos, that helps users understand DeFi concepts, the platform's features, and how to navigate the ecosystem.

Wallet Integration and Management: Enhanced UIs simplify the process of connecting popular wallets like "MetaMask", "Ledger", or "Trust Wallet". A one-click connection process with clear instructions helps reduce user friction. Allow users to view and manage their wallet balances, transaction history, and portfolio within the DEX interface. This reduces the need for users to switch between different applications.

Intuitive Trading Interface: Present token swaps in a clear and straightforward manner, with easy-to-use drop-down menus for selecting tokens, input fields for amounts, and a visible confirmation button. Display real-time market data, including price charts, trading volumes, and historical data, directly within the trading interface. Advanced users may appreciate additional tools like candlestick charts, order book depth, and indicators.

Transaction Summaries: Before confirming a trade, provide a detailed summary that includes the tokens being exchanged, the estimated gas fees, the expected slippage, and the final amount to be received. This transparency helps users make informed decisions. Fee Breakdown: Clearly display all fees involved in a transaction, including gas fees, platform fees, and any other applicable costs. This prevents users from being surprised by hidden charges.

Permission Warnings: Alert users when they are granting permissions to a smart contract, such as the ability to spend their tokens. Provide a clear explanation of what this means and any potential risks. Integrate scam detection tools that warn users if they are interacting with a known scam token or contract. These alerts can be based on community reports, on-chain analysis, or partnerships with security firms.

Mobile-Friendly Design: Ensure that the UI is fully responsive and optimized for mobile devices. As more users' access DeFi through mobile wallets, a seamless mobile experience is essential for retaining this user segment. Some DEXs may choose to offer dedicated mobile apps that provide the same functionality as the desktop platform, but with a design optimized for mobile interaction.

Cross-Platform Navigation: Enable seamless integration with other DeFi protocols and services, such as lending platforms, yield farming, or NFT marketplaces. This can be achieved through embedded links, widgets, or API integrations that allow users to access multiple DeFi services from a single interface. As the DeFi space expands across multiple blockchains, UIs should support multi-chain functionality, allowing users to easily switch between different networks (e.g., Ethereum, Binance Smart Chain, Polygon) without leaving the platform.

Examples of DEXs with Enhanced UIs

Uniswap Interface:
Overview: Uniswap's interface is known for its simplicity and ease of use, making it accessible even for newcomers to DeFi. The platform provides a clean and intuitive token swap interface, with minimal distractions and clear transaction details.

Key Features:

- Simple Swap Interface: Users can quickly select tokens, input amounts, and review transaction summaries.

- Slippage Tolerance Settings: Users can adjust slippage tolerance and transaction deadlines directly within the interface, providing flexibility while maintaining control over trades.

- Token Lists: Uniswap allows users to manage and customize token lists, ensuring they only interact with verified tokens.

SushiSwap Interface

SushiSwap has built an interface that not only supports token swaps but also integrates other DeFi functionalities like yield farming, staking, and lending within the same platform. This provides users with a comprehensive DeFi experience.

Key Features:

- Integrated DeFi Services: Users can easily navigate between swapping tokens, providing liquidity, staking SUSHI tokens, and borrowing or lending assets, all from the same dashboard.

- Interfoace provides users with detailed analytics on their positions, including APY calculations for yield farming and staking rewards.

- Users can personalize their experience by adjusting settings such as default currency displays and transaction preferences.

1inch Exchange

1inch is a decentralized exchange aggregator that finds the best prices across multiple DEXs. Its interface is designed to cater to both novice and advanced users, offering a range of trading tools and settings.

Key Features:

- Routing Optimization: The UI shows the optimal route for trades, including any potential savings from splitting the trade across multiple DEXs.

- For experienced users, 1inch offers advanced trading settings like partial fills, custom gas fees, and market depth analysis.
- The interface includes a gas price estimator that suggests the optimal gas fee based on network conditions, helping users avoid overpaying or underpaying for transactions.

Curve Finance Interface:

Curve Finance specializes in stablecoin trading and liquidity pools, and its interface is optimized for users focused on low-slippage trading. While the original interface was more functional than visually appealing, Curve has made improvements to enhance usability.

Key Features:

- The UI emphasizes low-slippage swaps between stablecoins, with clear indications of expected slippage and fees.
- Users can easily view and manage their liquidity positions, including deposit and withdrawal options, APYs, and pool statistics.

dYdX Interface:

dYdX is a DEX that focuses on derivatives and margin trading. Its interface is designed to cater to advanced traders who require detailed analytics, real-time data, and efficient order execution.

Key Features:

- The interface includes a comprehensive order book, advanced charting tools, and real-time price feeds, catering to traders who need in-depth market analysis.
- Users can customize their trading dashboard, adjusting the layout to display preferred trading pairs, order history, and performance metrics.

- Traders can manage their portfolio directly from the platform, with detailed insights into their open positions, margin balances, and collateral levels.

Challenges in Enhancing UIs for DeFi DEXs

Balancing Simplicity and Functionality:
While simplifying the UI for newcomers is essential, advanced users may require more detailed tools and analytics. Striking the right balance between simplicity and functionality can be challenging. Platforms must provide enough depth in features and customization options to satisfy experienced traders while maintaining an accessible interface for beginners.

Users have varying levels of experience and preferences. Offering customizable interfaces can address this but also adds complexity to the UI design and development. Ensuring that these interfaces remain intuitive and efficient requires thoughtful design and possibly the provision of templates or presets that cater to different user types.

Security and User Trust:

Simplifying the UI should not come at the cost of security. It is crucial to ensure that security features, such as permission warnings and scam alerts, are visible and comprehensible without overwhelming the user. This involves integrating these features seamlessly into the interface, perhaps with contextual help or simplified security dashboards that do not compromise the overall user experience.

New users may be hesitant to trust decentralized platforms with their funds. Providing clear and transparent information about the platform's operations, audits, and security measures is essential to building trust. This might include detailed but accessible documentation, user testimonials, and real-time transparency about operational status and updates.

Adapting to Rapid Changes in DeFi:

UIs must be adaptable to incorporate these changes quickly without disrupting the user experience. This may involve modular designs or the ability to update components of the UI without requiring significant downtime or learning curves for users.

As DeFi expands across multiple blockchains, integrating and managing cross-chain functionalities within a single UI can be complex. This requires robust back-end systems and an interface that can seamlessly switch contexts or chain environments. It might involve unified accounts or dashboards that aggregate information across chains and provide a consistent user experience regardless of the underlying blockchain technology.

The future of decentralized exchange interfaces in the DeFi ecosystem appears poised for transformative changes, with the integration of advanced technologies designed to enhance user engagement and simplify interactions. Here's a closer look at some key trends that could shape the development of these platforms:

AI-Driven Personalization: The integration of artificial intelligence and machine learning can significantly refine how users interact with DEX platforms by offering personalized experiences tailored to individual behaviors, preferences, and trading history. This could involve AI-curated views that highlight relevant trading opportunities, suggest optimal trading strategies, or even automate certain decision-making processes based on the user's past actions and market conditions.

Voice and Chat Interfaces: With advancements in voice recognition and natural language processing (NLP), DEXs could implement voice-activated commands or chat-based interfaces. This approach would make the platforms more accessible, especially for users who are less comfortable with traditional trading interfaces. Voice and chat interfaces could simplify tasks like executing trades, querying current market states, or setting up trading alerts, making the platforms more intuitive and user-friendly.

Virtual and Augmented Reality: The potential incorporation of virtual reality (VR) and augmented reality (AR) technologies offers an innovative way to interact with financial data and trading environments.

By using VR and AR, DEXs could create more engaging and immersive trading experiences, allowing users to visualize market trends.

These innovations could not only make DeFi more appealing to a broader audience but also enhance the efficiency and enjoyment of trading, potentially accelerating the adoption of DeFi platforms by mainstream finance users. As these technologies develop, they are likely to introduce new paradigms for interaction within the financial sector, significantly impacting how people manage and trade their assets in a decentralized manner.

Integration with Traditional Finance in DeFi DEXs:

The integration of Decentralized Exchanges with traditional financial systems represents a significant milestone in the evolution of DeFi. By bridging the gap between DeFi and traditional finance, this integration aims to create a more inclusive, efficient, and transparent global financial ecosystem. The collaboration between these two sectors can lead to hybrid models that combine the strengths of both worlds, offering regulated, secure, and scalable financial products and services.

Integration with traditional finance is crucial for DeFi and DEXs for several reasons that cater to broader market access, regulatory compliance, innovation, and stability:

Access to a Broader Market:

Integrating with traditional financial systems enables DeFi DEXs to attract a broader audience, including institutional investors, regulated entities, and retail investors who may be hesitant to engage with purely decentralized platforms. This is due to concerns around regulation and security inherent in DeFi.

Traditional financial institutions control vast amounts of capital. By bridging DeFi with traditional finance, this capital can flow into DeFi markets, enhancing liquidity, providing greater market depth, and potentially reducing volatility, which is beneficial for the overall health and growth of the DeFi sector.

Regulatory Compliance:

Adopting hybrid models that incorporate elements of regulatory compliance allows DEXs to offer products and services that conform to the legal frameworks of various jurisdictions. This adaptation can increase trust and participation from regulated financial entities, widening the user base and enhancing the legitimacy of DeFi services.

Integrating with traditional finance could bring stronger consumer protection measures to DeFi, such as insurance against losses, enhanced anti-fraud mechanisms, and adherence to anti-money laundering (AML) and know-your-customer (KYC) regulations, making these platforms safer and more secure for users.

Innovation and Product Development:

The convergence of DeFi and traditional finance can stimulate the creation of innovative financial products that leverage the strengths of both systems. This includes the development of tokenized real-world assets, decentralized derivatives markets, and hybrid models of lending that could offer improved returns and lower risks.

Traditional finance's extensive experience in risk management can be invaluable when integrated into DeFi platforms. This can lead to the development of more robust and secure financial products, potentially attracting more conservative investors who prioritize security.

Increased Trust and Stability:

The involvement of well-regulated and established financial institutions can enhance trust among investors and users, particularly those concerned with the speculative and sometimes unsecure nature of DeFi markets.

Integration with traditional finance can bring greater market stability by tempering the speculative dynamics of DeFi markets. It also introduces more sophisticated financial instruments and advanced risk management practices that can mitigate large-scale market manipulations or the impacts of high volatility.

Models for Integrating DeFi DEXs with Traditional Finance

Hybrid Financial Models: Hybrid models blend elements of decentralized finance (DeFi) and traditional finance (TradFi) to offer regulated financial products on decentralized platforms. These models often involve collaborations between DeFi protocols and traditional financial institutions, allowing for the creation of products that comply with regulatory standards while leveraging the efficiency and transparency of blockchain technology. Example: A decentralized exchange (DEX) might partner with a traditional bank to offer tokenized versions of traditional assets like bonds or equities. These tokenized assets would adhere to regulatory requirements such as Know Your Customer (KYC) and Anti-Money Laundering (AML), aligning with traditional finance standards.

Tokenized Real-World Assets: Tokenization converts real-world assets, like real estate or share of real estate, commodities, or securities, into digital tokens that can be traded on a blockchain. This process enhances the liquidity of traditionally illiquid assets and enables fractional ownership, broadening access to a wider range of investors. Example: A DEX could facilitate the trading of tokenized real estate share, enabling users to buy, sell, and trade these assets in a decentralized environment. For example, a token representing a share of a company asset could be traded on a DEX, providing decentralized access to traditional equity markets.

On-Ramps and Off-Ramps: On-ramps and off-ramps provide services that allow users to convert fiat currency to cryptocurrency and vice versa, facilitating participation in DeFi markets. These services are fundamental for bridging the gap between traditional finance and DeFi, enabling seamless transitions between the two systems. Example: A DEX might integrate with a licensed payment processor or exchange that offers fiat-to-crypto conversions, allowing users to deposit fiat currencies like USD or EUR directly into their wallets to trade on the DEX. Conversely, users could convert their cryptocurrency holdings back into fiat and withdraw them to their bank accounts.

DeFi-Compliant Stablecoins: How They Work: Stablecoins are digital assets pegged to the value of a fiat currency, such as the USD. DeFi-compliant stablecoins are designed to adhere to regulatory standards, making them suitable for use in both DeFi and traditional financial systems. Example: USD Coin (USDC) is a stablecoin backed by regulated financial institutions and audited regularly. It's utilized in various DeFi applications, including DEXs, for trading, lending, and as a medium of exchange. By integrating stablecoins like USDC, DEXs can provide a stable and familiar asset for traditional finance participants to engage with DeFi platforms.

Decentralized Identity and KYC/AML Compliance: Decentralized identity solutions allow users to verify their identities on the blockchain in a privacy-preserving way, enabling access to regulated financial products while maintaining control over personal data. These solutions can integrate with KYC/AML processes to satisfy regulatory demands. Example: A DEX might employ a decentralized identity protocol enabling users to complete KYC/AML checks once, then use their verified identity across multiple platforms without needing to repeatedly share their personal information. This capability can attract regulated financial entities and institutions that require adherence to these regulatory standards.

Challenges in DeFi-Traditional Finance Integration

Regulatory Uncertainty:

The regulatory landscape for decentralized finance (DeFi) is in flux, with jurisdictions worldwide adopting different stances on the regulation of digital assets and decentralized platforms. This uncertainty can pose challenges for DEXs that aspire to integrate with traditional finance, as it complicates strategic planning and compliance efforts.

Achieving compliance with diverse regulatory frameworks can be both costly and complex, particularly for decentralized platforms operating on a global scale. The expense and effort required to navigate these varying regulations can be significant, potentially limiting the ability of DEXs to expand and innovate.

Technical Integration: Successfully integrating decentralized platforms with traditional financial systems necessitates robust interoperability between blockchain technology and established financial infrastructure. This integration is technically challenging due to differences in standards, protocols, and data formats, which can hinder seamless connectivity.

As DeFi begins to intersect more with traditional finance, there could be a significant increase in transaction volumes and demand on blockchain networks. This raises concerns about scalability and network congestion, which could degrade performance and user experience.

Cultural Differences: Decentralization vs. Centralization: DeFi's foundational principles of decentralization, transparency, and permissionless access contrast sharply with the centralized and regulated framework of traditional finance. Bridging these distinct operational and philosophical approaches requires overcoming considerable cultural and operational differences.

Trust and Risk Management: Traditional financial institutions may be cautious about engaging with DeFi platforms due to concerns over counterparty risk, the potential for smart contract vulnerabilities, and the absence of a centralized authority to enforce agreements and resolve disputes.

User Experience:

Complexity of DeFi: Users accustomed to traditional finance may find DeFi platforms overly complex and challenging to navigate, especially if they are not familiar with the nuances of blockchain technology and the concept of self-custody of digital assets. Simplifying the user experience, providing educational resources, and enhancing interface design are crucial steps to attract and retain participants from the traditional finance sector. These improvements can help bridge the gap and make DeFi more accessible and appealing to a broader audience.

DeFi DEXs and Traditional Finance Integration Examples

Aave and Aave Arc:

Aave is a decentralized lending protocol that enables users to lend and borrow digital assets. Aave Arc, on the other hand, is a permissioned version of the Aave protocol designed specifically for institutional use, providing a compliant environment with mandatory KYC/AML checks.

Aave Arc facilitates the participation of traditional financial institutions in DeFi lending and borrowing while adhering to regulatory requirements. This setup bridges the gap between the decentralized liquidity of DeFi and the compliance needs of institutional investors, making it a crucial link for bringing established financial entities into the DeFi space.

Synthetix and Synthetic Assets: "Synthetix" is a DeFi protocol that enables the trading of synthetic assets, which are tokenized representations of real-world assets including commodities, fiat currencies, and stocks. Synthetix allows users to gain exposure to traditional financial markets without leaving the decentralized ecosystem by offering synthetic versions of traditional assets. This capability not only broadens access to global markets but also enhances liquidity and trading opportunities within the DeFi sector.

Compound Treasury:

Compound Treasury is a service from Compound Finance that provides institutions with the ability to earn a fixed interest rate on USD deposits. It is crafted to deliver the advantages of DeFi lending with the regulatory compliance and safety that traditional financial institutions require. Compound Treasury serves as a bridge for traditional financial institutions to engage with DeFi. It offers a simplified, compliant entry point into DeFi, enabling institutions to benefit from the yields of DeFi without the complexities and risks typically associated with managing crypto assets.

Circle and USDC:

Circle[49] is the company behind USDC, a regulated stablecoin that is pegged to and backed by US dollars, ensuring stability and reliability. USDC is extensively used in DeFi as a stable medium of exchange.

USDC serves as a vital conduit between DeFi and traditional finance, providing a stable and compliant digital currency that can be utilized across both decentralized platforms and traditional financial systems. Circle's partnerships with financial institutions and payment processors enhance this integration, enabling seamless transitions and broader acceptance and use of USDC in various financial operations.

Outlook for DeFi DEXs and Traditional Finance Integration

Institutional Adoption:

As the regulatory environment around DeFi becomes clearer and more DeFi protocols develop compliant products, institutional adoption is expected to rise. This would bring increased liquidity, improved pricing, and broader participation, thereby strengthening the overall market structure of DeFi decentralized exchanges (DEXs).

The ongoing collaboration between DeFi and traditional finance is poised to foster the creation of innovative financial products. These might include hybrid funds that combine elements of decentralized mechanisms with traditional investment structures, tokenized securities that offer new forms of investment opportunities on blockchain platforms, and decentralized insurance products that leverage smart contracts for claims processing and payouts.

Regulatory Clarity:

The establishment of global regulatory standards for digital assets and DeFi could greatly facilitate the integration of DEXs with traditional financial systems. Such standards would enable platforms to operate seamlessly across jurisdictions, reducing the operational risks and complexities associated with compliance.

Advances in technology will likely lead to the development of new tools and protocols for compliance, such as decentralized identity verification systems and automated KYC/AML processes. These tools will help bridge the gap between the open nature of DeFi and the regulated framework of TradFi.

---

[49] https://www.circle.com

Enhanced Security and Risk Management:

Incorporating traditional finance's risk management practices into DeFi protocols can lead to the creation of more secure and resilient financial products. Strategies such as hedging, diversification, and insurance could mitigate the inherent risks of DeFi platforms.

The demand for greater transparency within DeFi could be met with regular audits, standardized reporting, and more transparent operational processes. This would enhance trust and reliability, making DeFi platforms more appealing to traditional financial institutions and conservative investors.

User-Centric Design: To attract a mainstream audience, DeFi platforms are expected to continue focusing on simplifying user interfaces. This involves redesigning complex workflows into more user-friendly experiences, thus lowering the barrier to entry for traditional finance participants unfamiliar with blockchain technology.

As DeFi grows, the need for comprehensive education and effective onboarding programs becomes crucial. These programs will help users from the traditional finance sector understand and navigate the complexities of DeFi, ensuring they can effectively use and benefit from decentralized financial services.

The integration of DeFi DEXs with traditional finance represents a significant step toward a more inclusive, efficient, and innovative financial system. By bridging the gap between these two worlds, hybrid models and regulated offerings can unlock new opportunities for investors, enhance market liquidity, and create more robust and secure financial products. As the DeFi ecosystem continues to evolve, the collaboration between decentralized and traditional finance will play a crucial role in shaping the future of global finance.

Advanced Financial Instruments in DeFi DEXs

DEXs in the DeFi ecosystem have evolved beyond simple token swaps and now offer a range of advanced financial instruments that provide users with more sophisticated trading options. These instruments, including options, futures, and synthetic assets, allow traders to hedge risks, speculate on future price movements, and gain exposure to a wider array of assets. By introducing these features, DeFi DEXs are increasingly mirroring the complexity and functionality of traditional financial markets, but with the added benefits of decentralization, transparency, and accessibility. Here are some key advanced financial instruments in DeFi DEXs:

Options:

Options are financial derivatives that grant the holder the right, but not the obligation, to buy (call option) or sell (put option) an underlying asset at a predetermined price (strike price) before or on a specified date (expiration date).

Use Cases:

Hedging: Traders use options to hedge against potential adverse price movements in the underlying asset. For example, a trader holding ETH can buy a put option to protect against a potential decline in ETH's price.

Speculation: Traders can speculate on the price direction of an asset by purchasing call options if they believe the price will increase or put options if they anticipate a decrease.

DeFi Example:

Hegic[50]: Hegic is a decentralized options trading DeFi protocol on Ethereum that allows users to buy and sell call and put options on ETH and WBTC. The protocol automates these transactions through smart contracts, facilitating options trading without a central authority.

Futures:

Futures contracts are agreements to buy or sell an asset at a predetermined future date and price. Unlike options, futures obligate the parties to execute the trade at the specified expiration date.

Use Cases:

---

[50] https://www.hegic.co

Traders use futures to bet on the future price of an asset. For instance, a trader might enter a futures contract to buy ETH at a set price in the future, expecting the price to rise.

Futures are also used to hedge against price fluctuations. For example, a miner might sell futures contracts to lock in the price for Bitcoin they plan to mine in the future.

DeFi Example:

dYdX[51]: dYdX is a decentralized platform offering perpetual futures contracts, which are futures without an expiration date. This allows traders to take long or short positions on various cryptocurrencies with leverage, similar to trading on traditional financial exchanges.

Synthetic Assets:

Synthetic assets are tokenized ("Tokenized" refers to the process of converting assets, rights, or data into a digital token on a blockchain or distributed ledger) versions of real-world assets like stocks, commodities, fiat currencies, or other cryptocurrencies. They mimic the value of the underlying asset, providing exposure without direct ownership.

Use Cases:

Exposure to Traditional Markets: Synthetic assets enable DeFi users to access traditional financial markets, such as stock or commodity markets, within the blockchain ecosystem.

Cross-Asset Trading: Traders can create portfolios that include both synthetic assets and cryptocurrencies, diversifying their investments and accessing a broader market range.

DeFi Example:

Synthetix[52]: Synthetix is a DeFi protocol on Ethereum for creating and trading synthetic assets. Users can mint ("mint" refers to the process of

---

[51] https://dydx.exchange
[52] https://synthetix.io

creating new synthetic assets (Synths) on a blockchain by locking collateral (usually a cryptocurrency) in a smart contract) synthetic assets (known as Synths) that track the value of various real-world assets, using decentralized oracles (a service or system that provides external real-world data to smart contracts) for accurate price feeds.

Benefits of Advanced Financial Instruments in DeFi DEXs

The emergence and growth of sophisticated financial instruments in DeFi decentralized exchanges (DEXs) bring multiple transformative impacts on market dynamics, participation, and the variety of investment strategies available. Here are some key developments:

Increased Market Sophistication:

DeFi DEXs that offer options, futures, and synthetic assets enable traders to engage in complex trading strategies typically seen in traditional finance, such as hedging, arbitrage, and leveraging. These sophisticated tools help manage risks more effectively and exploit market inefficiencies, aligning DeFi more closely with established financial markets.

The availability of advanced financial instruments draws a wider range of participants, including institutional investors and professional traders who demand robust tools for risk management and opportunities to maximize returns. This broader participation not only increases the volume and liquidity of the markets but also enhances the maturity and stability of the DeFi ecosystem.

Improved Liquidity and Market Efficiency:

The inclusion of derivatives and synthetic assets in DeFi attracts liquidity providers drawn by the potential for trading fees and yield farming opportunities. This influx of liquidity improves market efficiency by reducing slippage and facilitating smoother and more reliable trade execution.

Advanced financial instruments improve price discovery mechanisms in DeFi markets by factoring in future price expectations and broader market sentiment. This enhancement helps align prices more closely with underlying economic fundamentals and market conditions, contributing to overall market efficiency.

Diversification of Investment Opportunities:

Synthetic assets provide DeFi users with access to traditional financial markets such as equities, commodities, and fiat currencies without needing to interact with traditional financial institutions or leave the blockchain ecosystem. This access facilitates a diversification of investment opportunities and lessens the dependency on volatile cryptocurrency markets alone.

By integrating traditional and crypto assets, traders can create more diversified and balanced portfolios. This diversification spreads risk across different asset classes and can potentially improve returns while minimizing exposure to adverse market movements.

DeFi Native Innovations:

DeFi leverages smart contracts to create financial products that are unfeasible in traditional finance. These include combining various derivatives into novel financial instruments, automating complex settlement processes, and engineering perpetual contracts without expiry dates. Such innovations showcase the unique capabilities of blockchain technology in reshaping financial products and services.

DeFi operates on principles of decentralization and contrasting sharply with traditional financial markets that often have barriers such as accreditation requirements or the need for intermediaries. In DeFi, anyone with internet access can participate, broadening financial inclusion and democratizing access to financial services.

Challenges of Advanced Instruments in DeFi DEXs

Navigating the complexities of advanced financial instruments in DeFi involves addressing multiple challenges ranging from user education to regulatory compliance and technical risks. Here's a detailed exploration of these challenges:

Complexity and User Education:

Advanced financial instruments like options, futures, and synthetic assets come with inherent complexities that many DeFi users may not initially understand. This complexity necessitates comprehensive educational initiatives and robust onboarding processes to help users grasp how these instruments function and how to use them effectively. This situation can be overcome by developing AI-based algorithms and teaching them to users.

There's a significant risk of loss associated with derivatives and synthetic assets, particularly if users misunderstand the risks involved. DeFi platforms need to provide transparent information and tools that help users understand and manage these risks, such as detailed risk assessments and scenario analyses.

Regulatory Uncertainty:

The use of derivatives and synthetic assets in DeFi introduces various regulatory issues, especially concerning securities laws, market manipulation, and investor protection. As regulatory frameworks for DeFi evolve, platforms dealing with these instruments must adeptly navigate the changing legal landscape, often adapting their operations to remain compliant.

Given that DeFi operates on a global scale, the diverse regulatory environments across different jurisdictions pose significant challenges. DeFi platforms must manage these varying requirements effectively, which is particularly difficult for decentralized entities without a central legal structure.

Smart Contract Risks:

The complex smart contracts that underpin operations involving options, futures, and synthetic assets heighten the risk of bugs or vulnerabilities, potentially leading to exploitations by malicious entities. Regular and thorough audits, along with stringent security protocols, are critical to mitigate these risks.

Many synthetic assets and derivatives rely on external data from oracles to function correctly. If these oracles deliver inaccurate data due to compromise or errors, they can cause significant disruptions, such as incorrect asset valuations or unwarranted liquidations, affecting market stability and user trust.

Liquidity Fragmentation:

As more synthetic assets and derivatives are introduced across various DeFi platforms, liquidity can become fragmented, diluting the market depth of each asset and potentially leading to higher trading costs and slippage. This fragmentation can reduce market efficiency and deter participation.

Ensuring that synthetic assets and derivatives are compatible and interoperable across different DeFi platforms poses a considerable technical challenge. As the ecosystem grows and new protocols and standards are developed, maintaining seamless compatibility becomes increasingly complex.

Governance and Decentralization in DeFi DEXs

Governance and decentralization are core principles of DEXs within the DeFi ecosystem. By increasing decentralization and implementing community governance models, DeFi protocols empower their users to have a direct say in the direction of the platform, including decisions about protocol upgrades, changes to fee structures, and the introduction of new features. This shift toward community-led governance aligns with the broader ethos of decentralization in DeFi, where no single entity controls the system, and decisions are made collectively by the stakeholders.

Governance and Decentralization in DeFi DEXs

Decentralized governance in DeFi platforms offers several transformative benefits that enhance user engagement, ensure greater system transparency and accountability, promote true decentralization, and drive continuous innovation. Here's a deeper look at these advantages:

Empowering Users:

Governance models in DeFi allow users to actively participate in decision-making processes. This democratization is a stark contrast to traditional centralized exchanges (CEXs), where decisions are typically made by a centralized authority without direct user involvement. In DeFi, users can vote on key issues, influencing the platform's development and operational policies.

By involving users in governance, DeFi platforms ensure that the interests of developers, users, and other stakeholders are more closely aligned. This participatory approach helps ensure that the platform evolves in ways that are beneficial to the broader community, fostering a sense of ownership and commitment among its members. On the other hand, adopting this participatory governance blockchain models in traditional finance could enhance stakeholder alignment, foster community engagement, and drive more inclusive decision-making processes.

Ensuring Transparency and Accountability:

Decentralized governance is characterized by transparent voting mechanisms. All proposals, discussions, and voting outcomes are made public, ensuring that every action taken is visible and open for scrutiny. This level of transparency promotes accountability, as community members can see how decisions are made and by whom. This openness allows the community to hold developers and decision-makers accountable. It reduces the risk of corruption, misuse of power, or misallocation of resources, which are more prevalent in opaque or centralized systems.

Encouraging Decentralization:

Decentralized governance structures minimize the concentration of power within a single entity or a small group of individuals. This is crucial for maintaining the trust and integrity of DeFi platforms, as it ensures that no single party can unilaterally make decisions that could compromise the platform's objectives or security.

The decentralized nature of governance makes DeFi platforms inherently more resistant to external pressures or censorship from regulators or malicious actors. This resilience is critical in maintaining the platform's independence and uninterrupted operation under various conditions.

Driving Innovation and Adaptation:

In a decentralized governance model, innovation is primarily driven by community needs and feedback. Users are encouraged to propose new features, enhancements, or protocol adjustments. This can lead to more rapid and relevant innovations, keeping the platform at the forefront of technological advancement.

The ability to propose and vote on changes swiftly allows DeFi platforms to adapt quickly to new challenges, market conditions, or opportunities. This agility is often lacking in more traditional, centralized systems where changes can be slow and bogged down by bureaucratic processes.

Common Governance Models in DeFi DEXs

Decentralized exchanges (DEXs) and other DeFi platforms utilize various governance models to engage community participation and ensure decentralized decision-making. Here's an overview of some prominent governance models used in DeFi:

Token-Based Governance:

In token-based governance, the voting power is usually proportional to the number of governance tokens a user holds. These tokens can be native to the platform and might be acquired through purchasing, earning via participation, or as rewards. Example: Uniswap's UNI Token: Uniswap, a DEX, uses its UNI token for governance purposes. Holders of UNI can propose changes, vote on different proposals, and delegate their voting power to other users or representatives, making it a direct way for stakeholders to influence the platform's development and policy.

DAO-Based Governance:

Decentralized Autonomous Organizations (DAOs) represent a structure where the community governs a protocol via collective decision-making. Governance through DAOs is executed using smart contracts, which automate processes and ensure that the outcomes of votes are implemented. Example: MakerDAO[53], a decentralized lending platform, uses its MKR tokens for governance. MKR holders have the authority to make key decisions concerning the protocol, such as adjustments in the stability fee, decisions about acceptable collateral types, and risk management parameters.

Quadratic Voting:

Quadratic voting[54] is a method that aims to democratize influence by making the cost of casting votes increase quadratically with the number of votes cast[55]. This approach reduces the ability of large holders to dominate decisions due to the increasing cost of buying more votes. Example: CityDAO utilizes quadratic voting[56] to allow its members to express the intensity of their preferences on various proposals, ensuring that decisions reflect the collective will of the community while mitigating the influence of large stakeholders. This approach promotes more democratic and equitable governance within the organization.

Multi-Signature (Multi-Sig) Governance:

Multi-signature governance[57] involves multiple parties to approve a transaction or change before it can be executed. This type of governance is often used to enhance security and oversight, especially in conjunction with other governance models like DAOs or token-based systems. Example: "Gnosis Safe[58]" is widely used among DeFi projects as a multi-signature wallet for managing funds and protocol decisions. It

---

[53] https://makerdao.com/en/governance
[54] https://pepi.codes/blog/2024-09-07
[55] https://blog.colony.io/what-is-quadratic-voting-a-guide-to-dao-decision-making/
[56] https://www.belfercenter.org/sites/default/files/2024-08/CaseStudy_TAPP_CityDAO_Helena_Rong.pdf
[57] https://www.techtarget.com/searchcio/definition/multisig-multisignature
[58] https://www.gnosis.io

requires a pre-determined number of signatures from trusted community members or elected signatories before implementing significant changes or transactions.

Governance Processes and Features in DeFi DEXs

The governance processes in decentralized finance (DeFi) are designed to engage community participation and ensure transparent, equitable decision-making. Here's a breakdown of the key stages in the governance lifecycle in DeFi protocols:

Proposal Creation:

Typically, anyone holding a requisite amount of governance tokens or members of a DAO can submit proposals. This threshold is meant to ensure that proposers have a vested interest in the protocol's success.

Proposals can vary widely, covering aspects from technical upgrades, such as improvements to smart contract codes, to financial adjustments like fee structures, and even strategic decisions including partnerships and product expansions.

Voting Mechanisms:

In token-based governance systems, an individual's voting power is usually proportional to the number of governance tokens they hold. Many systems also allow users to delegate their voting rights to others, effectively enabling a representative form of governance.

Quorum Requirements[59]: To ensure that decisions reflect the community's will, many governance systems require that a minimum percentage of voting power participate in a vote for the results to be valid which is known as meeting a quorum.

There is predefined voting periods during which votes can be cast. Once this period ends, votes are tallied, and the proposal is either approved or rejected based on the majority decision.

---

[59]https://blog.colony.io/quorum-in-dao-voting-ensuring-decisive-and-representative-decisions/

Execution of Decisions:

For many DeFi platforms, if a proposal is approved, it is "automatically executed" via smart contracts. This automation ensures that the implementation of decisions is timely and reduces the risk of human error or interference.

Some decisions, particularly those involving complex or external actions, require "manual implementation". These are usually managed by trusted community members or executed through a multi-signature wallet arrangement to maintain security and integrity.

Transparency and Documentation:

The transparency in DeFi governance is notable, with all proposals, discussions, voting records, and outcomes publicly recorded on the blockchain. This level of openness allows anyone to audit the process and ensures accountability.

Robust governance is supported by active community engagement on various platforms, such as dedicated governance forums. These forums serve as a venue for discussion, collaboration, and consensus-building, ensuring that a wide range of perspectives are considered.

Examples of DeFi DEXs with Governance Models

Uniswap (UNI Governance)

Uniswap is a DEX known for its efficiency and ease of use, leveraging its native token, UNI, for governance. UNI holders can create governance proposals if they hold or have delegated a threshold of at least 1% of the total UNI supply. Before voting, proposals typically undergo a discussion phase in community forums. UNI holders may vote on proposals directly or delegate their voting rights to other users. Voting power is proportional to the number of UNI tokens held. Key decisions include protocol upgrades, like the introduction of Uniswap V3, and strategic initiatives regarding UNI token distribution.

MakerDAO (MKR Governance)

MKR holders vote on crucial risk parameters, including types of accepted collateral, stability fees, and debt ceilings, affecting the overall stability and operation of the DAI ecosystem. MKR holders can initiate an emergency shutdown in critical situations to protect the system's integrity. Governance actions have included the integration of new collateral types and adjustments to DAI's savings rate, particularly in response to market fluctuations.

SushiSwap (SUSHI Governance)

Originating as a fork of Uniswap, SushiSwap has differentiated itself with unique features and a distinct governance model using the SUSHI token. SUSHI token holders can propose and vote on various changes ranging from protocol upgrades to marketing strategies. The protocol's funds are managed through a multi signature wallets, which requires multiple signatories to approve expenditures, ensuring that treasury funds are spent on community-approved initiatives. Notable governance outcomes include the creation of SushiBar[60], where users can stake SUSHI, and the launch of BentoBox[61], a vault system (a system refers to a set of smart contracts designed to manage and optimize the use of digital assets) for various DeFi applications.

Compound (COMP Governance)

Compound is a decentralized lending platform where users can supply and borrow cryptocurrencies, governed by COMP token[62] holders. Holders with at least 100,000 COMP can submit proposals that often pertain to protocol modifications, such as adjustments to interest rate models or the addition of new lending markets. Proposals that meet the minimum voting threshold and achieve a quorum are automatically implemented by the protocol. Decisions have included the inclusion of new collateral assets and updates to risk parameters and interest models. These platforms illustrate the diverse approaches to DeFi governance, highlighting the importance of community involvement and the

---

[60] https://www.gemini.com/cryptopedia/sushiswap-sushi-coin-sushibar-chef-nomi#section-sushi-swap-overview-and-origin
[61] https://www.sushi.com/academy/products/bentobox
[62] https://compound.finance

innovative use of smart contracts to facilitate decentralized administration and continuous protocol evolution.

Challenges in Governance and Decentralization

The following is a comprehensive analysis of prevalent challenges in DeFi governance along with proposed strategies for their resolution:

Concentration of Voting Power:

Whale[63] Influence: In token-based governance systems, large holders, often called "whales" can disproportionately influence decisions, potentially leading to outcomes that favor a minority at the expense of the broader community.

To counteract the concentration of power, some platforms explore methods like quadratic voting, which increases the cost of votes exponentially with the number of votes cast. This method aims to balance influence among all participants. Additionally, staking mechanisms can be employed where the influence of a user's vote may be linked to the duration or quantity of tokens staked, rather than just the number of tokens held.

Low Voter Participation:

A common issue in DeFi governance is "low voter turnout", where only a small fraction of token holders participates in decision-making. This can lead to a scenario where a handful of active participants "dictate" governance outcomes.

Platforms might offer incentives like token rewards for participating in votes or special governance tokens that can improve engagement. Educational and engagement campaigns are also crucial in improving participation by making the process more accessible and understandable to holders.

Complexity of Proposals:

---

[63] https://www.coinbase.com/learn/crypto-basics/what-are-crypto-whales

The technical nature of proposals can deter average users from participating due to the difficulty in understanding the implications of decisions. To address this, platforms can provide simplified explanations, summaries, and risk-benefit analyses alongside proposals to help users make more informed decisions.

Governance Attacks:

Malicious Proposals[64]: Governance systems are susceptible to attacks where malicious actors, potentially through accumulating significant voting power, push through harmful proposals, especially in environments with low participation.

Implementing safeguards such as delaying the execution of proposals to allow for community review or requiring multi-signature verification for critical decisions can help mitigate these risks.

By empowering users through community-driven governance models, DeFi DEXs can foster more transparent, accountable, and user-focused platforms. While challenges like voter participation and power concentration persist, ongoing innovations in governance models and a commitment to progressive decentralization are likely to improve the resilience and sustainability of these platforms.

---

[64] https://metana.io/blog/governance-attacks-in-smart-contracts/

Lending and Borrowing Platforms

Lending and borrowing platforms are a cornerstone of DeFi ecosystem. These platforms allow users to lend their cryptocurrency assets to others and earn interest on these assets, or borrow against their crypto holdings, usually by providing collateral that exceeds the loan value. This setup creates a trustless environment for lending and borrowing, without the need for a traditional bank or financial institution.

Key Features:

Collateralization: Borrowers must over-collateralize their loans, meaning they must deposit more value in crypto assets than they borrow to protect lenders against the high volatility in the crypto markets.

Interest Rates: Rates are typically dynamic, adjusting based on supply and demand for the borrowed asset.

Decentralization: Transactions and interest calculations are managed through smart contracts on the blockchain.

Examples of DeFi Lending and Borrowing Platforms:

Aave: A DeFi lending platform that offers a variety of cryptocurrencies for lending and borrowing. Users can engage in stable and variable rate loans.

Compound: Another leading DeFi platform where users can supply crypto assets to earn interest or borrow against their holdings.

MakerDAO: Primarily focused on the creation of its stablecoin, DAI, which is backed by over-collateralized deposits of other crypto assets.

DeFi lending and borrowing platforms offer dynamic and automated interest rates influenced by market demand and supply, providing a decentralized framework where users can engage in financial activities directly through blockchain technology without traditional intermediaries.

Lending Rates for USDC:

Aave: Offers up to 7.33% APY on USDC lending[65] (12.2024). This rate adjusts based on the current market conditions, reflecting the demand and supply dynamics on the platform

"Compound" typically sets its interest rates[66] (10.6% APY 12.2024) algorithmically based on supply and demand. This system ensures that rates are continually updated to reflect market conditions

Considerations When Using DeFi Platforms for Lending and Borrowing:

DeFi relies on smart contract technology, which can introduce risks such as vulnerabilities or bugs. Unlike centralized platforms, DeFi doesn't typically offer customer support, making it crucial for users to understand the technology and platform operations thoroughly.

Rates are subject to significant fluctuations due to the inherent volatility in the crypto markets. This can affect returns, and the stability of assets lent or borrowed.

The lack of regulatory oversight in DeFi can pose additional risks and uncertainties compared to more traditional financial systems that are regulated and offer some level of consumer protection.

For users interested in participating in DeFi lending and borrowing, staying informed through platforms that offer real-time comparisons and updates, such as Bitcompare[67], is crucial to navigate this rapidly evolving sector effectively

Details of Lending and Borrowing Platforms

These platforms allow users to lend out their crypto assets in exchange for interest (called staking) or borrow assets by providing collateral, all through smart contracts without the need for traditional financial intermediaries like banks.

---

[65] https://bitcompare.net/platforms/aave/lending-rates
[66] https://exponential.fi/app
[67] https://bitcompare.net/staking-rewards

How Lending and Borrowing Platforms Work

Lending and borrowing platforms in DeFi utilize smart contracts to automate and enforce loan terms without the need for intermediaries.

Lending Process

Deposit: Lenders add their cryptocurrency to a lending platform's smart contract.

Earning Interest: The deposited assets are pooled with those from other users, allowing the lender to earn interest depending on how much demand there is to borrow those assets.

Interest Rate: Interest rates can be either fixed or variable, influenced by the platform's design and the current demand for the asset.

Withdrawal: Lenders can withdraw their assets along with any interest earned whenever they choose, subject to the terms of the platform.

Borrowing Process

Collateralization: Borrowers must provide cryptocurrency as collateral, usually valued at more than the loan amount they seek, a practice known as over-collateralization.

Borrowing: Borrowers can take out a loan of a different cryptocurrency, up to a limit set by the collateral's value.

Interest Payments: Borrowers accrue interest on the amount they borrow over time.

Repayment: To reclaim their collateral, borrowers must repay the borrowed sum along with any interest that has accrued.

Liquidation: If the market value of the collateral dips below a certain level, the smart contract may automatically liquidate the collateral to settle the debt.

These processes highlight the decentralized nature of DeFi platforms, which aim to offer more flexibility and efficiency compared to traditional financial systems.

Types of Lending and Borrowing Platforms

DeFi lending and borrowing platforms offer various innovative finance services, each tailored to different financial needs and risk profiles:

Collateralized Lending Platforms

These platforms are the backbone of DeFi lending, requiring borrowers to lock in cryptocurrency as collateral that surpasses the loan's value. This collateralization secures the loan and mitigates the risk of default from the borrower's side.

> Example: "Compound" allows users to deposit cryptocurrencies such as ETH or DAI and borrow against these holdings. This type of lending protects lenders by ensuring that loans are backed by more than their worth, providing a buffer against market volatility and default.

Flash Loan Platforms

Flash loans represent an innovative DeFi concept where loans are issued and repaid in the span of a single transaction block, without the need for collateral. These are typically used for arbitrage, swapping collateral, or quick financial maneuvers that can be settled instantly.

> Example: Aave enables users to borrow cryptocurrency instantaneously, with the stipulation that the loan must be repaid by the end of the transaction block. This facilitates operations like arbitrage between exchanges, where a quick buy and sell can cover the loan and potentially turn a profit within the same block.

Interest Rate Derivatives

Some platforms focus on "derivatives" that allow users to manage or hedge against the fluctuating interest rates in the DeFi market. These derivatives are financial instruments deriving their value from the underlying interest rates, offering ways to lock in rates or speculate on their movements.

> Example: Notional Finance[68] provides a platform where users can lock in fixed interest rates for lending or borrowing. This is particularly useful in a market known for its volatility, as it offers stability and predictability for financial planning.

Each type of platform caters to different aspects of financial management in the DeFi ecosystem, from risk mitigation and loan security with collateralized lending to sophisticated financial strategies enabled by flash loans and interest rate derivatives.

Benefits of DeFi Lending and Borrowing Platforms

Lending and borrowing platforms in DeFi offer several advantages over traditional financial services:

Global Accessibility DeFi platforms are accessible to anyone with an internet connection and some cryptocurrency, regardless of location, credit score, or banking status. This inclusivity is particularly beneficial in regions where traditional banking infrastructure is lacking or non-existent, allowing users from these areas to participate in global financial markets. For instance, users in countries with underdeveloped financial systems can engage in lending and borrowing activities on platforms.

Higher Interest Rates for Lenders Compared to traditional bank savings accounts, DeFi platforms often provide significantly higher interest rates. This is especially true in markets with high demand for certain cryptocurrencies. For example, lending DAI on a platform like Compound can yield much higher returns than what would be possible through savings accounts at conventional banks.

The operations of DeFi platforms are conducted on blockchain technology, which records all transactions and smart contract activities.

---

[68] https://www.notional.finance

This transparency[69] allows users to monitor and verify the flow of funds and the adjustment of interest rates in real-time, such as on Compound, where every transaction is openly documented and available for scrutiny.

Efficient Collateralization DeFi lending often involves over-collateralization, where borrowers must deposit more value in crypto assets than the amount they borrow. This method try to minimizes the risk of loss for lenders. If the market value of the collateral drops to a threshold where it no longer covers the loan, the smart contracts governing these platforms automatically initiate the liquidation of the borrower's assets to repay the debt, securing the lender's investment.

Risks and Challenges

While DeFi lending and borrowing platforms offer unique advantages, they also entail several risks that participants need to manage carefully:

The very foundation of DeFi platforms, smart contracts, can contain vulnerabilities or bugs that malicious actors might exploit, leading to losses. In August 2021, Poly Network, a decentralized finance platform, suffered a significant breach due to vulnerabilities in its smart contracts. In March 2022, the Ronin Network, an Ethereum sidechain developed for the NFT-based game Axie Infinity, suffered a significant breach due to compromised private keys. In December 2021, the decentralized finance platform BadgerDAO suffered a front-end attack that led to the loss of user funds. In May 2023, Level Finance, a decentralized finance platform on the BNB Chain, suffered a security breach due to vulnerabilities in its referral reward system's business logic and calculation methods. In February 2022, the Wormhole protocol, a cross-chain bridge facilitating asset transfers between different blockchains, suffered a significant security breach due to a smart contract vulnerability. In July 2024, LI.FI, a cross-chain decentralized finance (DeFi) platform, experienced a security breach due to a smart contract vulnerability. In May 2021, the decentralized exchange PancakeSwap experienced a DNS hijacking attack, where users were redirected to a malicious website that prompted them to enter their private keys. In September 2024, DeltaPrime, a decentralized finance platform operating

---

[69] https://etherscan.io

on the Arbitrum network, suffered a significant security breach due to an admin key hack.

Liquidity Risk In times of high demand or market volatility, there might not be enough liquidity on a platform, which can make it difficult for users to withdraw their funds or efficiently liquidate collateral. For instance, during a market crash, the sudden surge in demand for liquidations can lead to a liquidity crunch, where the platform cannot process transactions quickly enough, causing high slippage and further losses. In March 2020, during a significant market downturn, the decentralized finance (DeFi) platform MakerDAO faced a liquidity crisis. The rapid decline in Ethereum's price led to a surge in collateral liquidations. In November 2022, the decentralized finance (DeFi) platform Aave encountered a significant liquidity challenge when a trader attempted to short the CRV token by borrowing a substantial amount and selling it to drive down its price. In May 2022, the Terra blockchain experienced a catastrophic collapse when its algorithmic stablecoin, TerraUSD (UST), lost its peg to the U.S. dollar. This de-pegging led to a rapid decline in the value of its sister token, LUNA, causing both tokens to plummet in value. In June 2021, DeFi platform Iron Finance experienced a liquidity crisis with its partially collateralized stablecoin, IRON. A sudden surge in redemptions led to a "bank run," causing IRON to lose its peg to the U.S. dollar. In June 2022, Celsius Network, a prominent cryptocurrency lending platform, faced a severe liquidity crisis. Amidst extreme market conditions, the platform paused all customer withdrawals to stabilize operations. In September 2021, the DeFi platform SushiSwap faced a liquidity crisis during the launch of its token offering, MISO. A vulnerability in the platform's smart contract code was exploited, allowing an attacker to withdraw ETH. In March 2020, during a significant market downturn, the DeFi platform "Compound" faced liquidity challenges. In November 2022, the cryptocurrency exchange FTX faced a severe liquidity crisis following a sudden surge in customer withdrawals, which the platform was unable to fulfill due to insufficient liquid assets.

The volatile nature of cryptocurrencies means that the value of the collateral can dramatically fluctuate, increasing the risk of liquidation if the market moves unfavorably. For example, if someone borrows DAI using ETH as collateral and the price of ETH plummets, the borrower may face liquidation if the collateral's value falls below a certain threshold. In May 2021, Ethereum's price experienced a sharp decline from approximately $4,300 to $1,900 within a week. This significant drop led to substantial liquidations across various DeFi platforms, as the value of collateralized assets like ETH fell below required thresholds, triggering automatic sell-offs to cover outstanding debts.

The regulatory landscape for DeFi is still evolving, and there is a significant uncertainty regarding how stringent regulations might become. Potential regulatory changes could impact DeFi operations, possibly requiring platforms to implement KYC/AML processes or restricting access to certain jurisdictions. In December 2023, KuCoin[70], a cryptocurrency exchange, agreed to a settlement with the New York Attorney General's office for operating without proper registration and failing to implement required KYC and AML protocols.

Interest Rate Volatility Interest rates in DeFi platforms are subject to rapid changes based on market dynamics of supply and demand. This can pose challenges for both borrowers and lenders as they may see the interest rates on loans or deposits fluctuate more frequently and significantly than in traditional finance. For example, borrowers might see interest rates spike unexpectedly, which can increase the cost of borrowing unexpectedly. In October 2021, Aave, a DeFi platform, experienced significant interest rate volatility[71] for USDT borrowing. The variable interest rate surged from 3.73% to 61% within a single day (October 29–30, 2021).

---

[70]https://www.reuters.com/legal/crypto-exchange-kucoin-shut-new-york-pay-22-mln-settle-lawsuit-2023-12-12/
[71]https://blog.ipor.io/cream-exploit-is-aave-bank-run-an-over-reaction-77ebde45e52

Stablecoins

Stablecoins are a type of cryptocurrency designed to maintain a stable value by being pegged to a more stable asset, typically a widely recognized fiat currency like the US dollar. This pegging mechanism is critical as it aims to combine the best aspects of cryptocurrencies (such as security, privacy, and the ability to transact digitally) with the stable value of fiat currencies, which are less susceptible to the kind of volatility seen in traditional cryptocurrencies like Bitcoin or Ethereum.

Examples of Stablecoins

USDC (USD Coin): This is a fiat-collateralized stablecoin, each unit of which is backed by one US dollar held in reserve. USDC is widely used in the cryptocurrency market for trading, lending, and as a stable store of value.

DAI: Unlike USDC, DAI is an example of a crypto-collateralized stablecoin. It is backed by a mix of other cryptocurrencies that are deposited into smart contract vaults whenever new DAI is minted. The value of DAI is pegged to the US dollar and is kept stable through a dynamic system of collateralized debt positions (CDPs), autonomous feedback mechanisms, and appropriately incentivized external actors.

Use Cases in DeFi Stablecoins play a critical role in the DeFi ecosystem. They are frequently used to:

- Provide a safe haven from volatility in cryptocurrency markets.
- Facilitate trades between different cryptocurrencies without needing to convert back to fiat.
- Serve as a standard of value for quoting prices in DeFi platforms.
- Enable lending and borrowing services where they act as a predictable and stable unit of account.

Stablecoins like USDC and DAI have become fundamental components of the DeFi landscape, allowing users to engage in complex financial activities without the usual risks associated with high volatility in traditional cryptocurrencies. Examples of stablecoins include Tether (USDT), USD Coin (USDC), TrueUSD (TUSD), Pax Dollar (USDP), Binance USD (BUSD), Gemini Dollar (GUSD), Frax (FRAX), and Tether Gold (XAUT).

Definition and Basic Concepts

Stablecoins play a crucial role in the cryptocurrency ecosystem, particularly in DeFi, where they provide a reliable medium of exchange, a unit of account, and a store of value. A stablecoin is a type of cryptocurrency that aims to maintain a stable value relative to a reference asset, usually a fiat currency like the US dollar (USD), the euro (EUR), or a commodity like gold.

Types of Stablecoins

Stablecoins have become integral to the cryptocurrency market by providing price stability amidst the typically volatile environment of digital currencies. There are three primary types of stablecoins (fiat-collateralized, crypto-collateralized, and algorithmic (non-collateralized) stablecoins), each relying on different mechanisms to maintain their peg, typically to a fiat currency like the US dollar:

Fiat-Collateralized Stablecoins: These stablecoins are directly backed by fiat currency reserves, such as USD, held by a trusted custodian or in a bank account. This backing maintains a 1:1 ratio; for every stablecoin issued, there is a corresponding fiat unit held in reserve. For example, Tether (USDT) and USD Coin (USDC) are prominent fiat-collateralized stablecoins. The redemption process involves the user returning the stablecoin to the issuer, who then burns (destroys) the stablecoin and releases the equivalent fiat from the reserve to the user, thus maintaining the currency's stability.

Crypto-Collateralized Stablecoins: These stablecoins use other cryptocurrencies as collateral instead of fiat. Given the volatility of cryptocurrencies, these stablecoins are typically over-collateralized. This means the value of the cryptocurrency held in reserve exceeds the value of the stablecoins issued to ensure they remain fully backed even if the collateral's market price drops. DAI is a notable example of a crypto-collateralized stablecoin, primarily backed by Ethereum and other digital assets. Users lock up more cryptocurrency in value than the DAI they wish to generate, which is managed through smart contracts to maintain the necessary collateralization ratio. Another example of a crypto-collateralized stablecoin is "sUSD", developed by "Synthetix"[72], which maintains its value by being backed by a pool of various cryptocurrencies. Users can mint "sUSD" by locking up SNX tokens as collateral, with the system requiring over-collateralization to account for potential volatility in the underlying assets. Another example of a crypto-collateralized stablecoin is Reserve Rights[73] (RSV), which is backed by a basket of cryptocurrencies to maintain its value stability. The Reserve protocol employs a diversified collateral pool and an arbitrage mechanism to ensure RSV's peg to the U.S. dollar, aiming to provide a decentralized and inflation-resistant stablecoin solution.

<u>Algorithmic (Non-Collateralized) Stablecoins:</u> Algorithmic stablecoins do not have any physical or crypto assets backing them. Instead, they rely on "algorithms" and "smart contracts" to adjust the supply of the stablecoin based on changes in its market price to stabilize its value. TerraUSD (UST) are examples of such stablecoins. These algorithms automatically increase the supply when the stablecoin's price is above the target peg, aiming to reduce the price, and decrease the supply when the price is below the peg, aiming to increase the price. Another example of an algorithmic stablecoin is Basis Cash (BAC), which aimed to maintain its peg to the U.S. dollar through a seigniorage shares system involving multiple tokens. However, like TerraUSD (UST), Basis Cash struggled to maintain its peg, leading to significant devaluation and raising concerns about the reliability of algorithmic mechanisms in ensuring price stability. These stablecoins require a consistent level of demand to function effectively. A sudden drop in demand can disrupt the algorithm's ability to maintain the peg, leading to price instability. The stability often depends on independent actors engaging in arbitrage to correct price deviations. If arbitrageurs are absent or market conditions

---

[72] https://blog.synthetix.io/transitioning-to-synthetix-v3-scaling-susd-migrating-snx/
[73] https://reserve.org

hinder arbitrage opportunities, the stablecoin may fail to maintain its intended value[74].

How Stablecoins Work

The "stability mechanisms" of stablecoins are vital in maintaining their value close to a predetermined peg, typically to a stable asset like the US dollar. Here's how different types of stablecoins manage stability:

Pegging Mechanism: Stablecoins use a pegging mechanism to ensure their value remains consistent with a reference asset, often employing market-driven strategies such as "arbitrage" to achieve this. For example, if USDT (a fiat-collateralized stablecoin) trades below one dollar, arbitrageurs might buy it at a discount and redeem it for $1 in fiat currency, making a profit. This activity helps drive the price of USDT back to its pegged value of $1.

Redemption and Issuance: In fiat-collateralized stablecoins, the stability is managed through direct redemption and issuance processes. Users can exchange stablecoins for an "equivalent amount of fiat (such as USD)" directly from the issuer, who then burns the redeemed stablecoins to prevent inflation and maintain the currency peg. For instance, if someone redeems 1,000 USDC, the issuer will destroy these tokens and transfer $1,000 from their fiat reserves to the user, keeping the supply in balance with the backing reserves.

Collateralization Ratios: Crypto-collateralized stablecoins require users to "over-collateralize" their holdings to issue stablecoins. This method involves depositing a higher value of another cryptocurrency as security to account for price volatility. For example, to mint $100 worth of DAI, a user might need to lock up $150 worth of Ethereum. If the market value of the collateral (Ethereum, in this case) falls significantly, the system may automatically sell some of the collateral to preserve the stablecoin's value and maintain its peg.

Supply Adjustments: Algorithmic stablecoins control their peg by automatically adjusting the supply of tokens in circulation, based on

---

[74] https://www.theblock.co/learn/251858/algorithmic-stablecoins-what-is-pegging-and-how-are-they-unique

real-time market conditions. If the stablecoin's price exceeds the peg, the supply is increased to reduce its price. Conversely, if the price falls below the peg, the supply is decreased. An example is AMPL[75] (This platofrom employs a daily "rebase" mechanism to adjust its supply based on market demand), which adjusts its supply daily: if the price is above $1, the supply increases, distributing more tokens to holders, which should theoretically decrease the price back to the peg.

Fiat-Collateralized Stablecoins

Fiat-collateralized stablecoins are designed to offer stability in the highly volatile cryptocurrency market by being directly backed by traditional fiat currency reserves. This type of stablecoin maintains a peg to a fiat currency such as the US dollar or Euro, ensuring each coin in circulation is "matched" by an equivalent amount of fiat currency held in reserve. Below is a explanation of the functioning of fiat-collateralized stablecoins:

Backing Mechanism and Reserve System:

Fiat-collateralized stablecoins are backed by actual fiat currency reserves, which can be held in cash or cash-equivalent assets like treasury bills. These reserves are managed either by the stablecoin issuer or a trusted third party. The 1:1 backing aims to maintain a stable value pegged to the fiat currency, shielding these stablecoins from the usual cryptocurrency volatility. To ensure transparency and build trust, these reserves are typically audited by reputable third parties, confirming their existence and adequacy to cover the issued stablecoins.

Examples of Fiat-Collateralized Stablecoins

Tether (USDT): Tether, one of the most well-known stablecoins, claims each USDT token is backed by one US dollar held in reserve. However, Tether has faced scrutiny and legal challenges regarding the transparency and composition of its reserves. In 2021, the CFTC imposed a penalty on Tether for providing inaccurate statements regarding the composition of its reserves.

---

[75] https://www.ampleforth.org

USD Coin (USDC): USDC is managed by a consortium that includes Circle and Coinbase, emphasizing compliance and transparency in its operations. Each USDC is similarly backed by a dollar in reserve.

Issuance and Redemption Process:

To obtain fiat-collateralized stablecoins, a user typically deposits a corresponding amount of fiat currency with the issuer or a custodian. The issuer then mints an equivalent amount of stablecoins and disburses them to the user.

Users can redeem their stablecoins for fiat currency by returning them to the issuer, who then burns the returned tokens and releases the equivalent fiat from the reserves, maintaining the currency peg.

Maintaining Stability and Value:

The primary advantage of fiat-collateralized stablecoins is their stability, derived from direct backing by tangible, relatively stable fiat currencies. Unlike their crypto-collateralized or algorithmic counterparts, these stablecoins rely on a straightforward mechanism. Regular audits and publicly available reserve reports further bolster user confidence in these stablecoins.

Benefits and Risks:

These stablecoins offer a predictable and stable store of value, ease of transaction across borders, and straightforward redemption processes. The centralization of reserve management introduces risks related to trust in the issuer's ability to maintain sufficient reserves. Additionally, these stablecoins are subject to regulatory scrutiny which can impact their operation and viability.

Backing Mechanism of Fiat-Collateralized Stablecoins

The backing mechanism and reserve system of fiat-collateralized stablecoins rely on a robust framework to ensure each stablecoin in circulation has a corresponding fiat unit in reserve. This setup involves strict regulatory compliance, transparent audits, and precise mechanisms for managing the reserves and issuance of stablecoins.

Custodial Arrangements for Fiat Reserves:

Reserve Holding Institutions: The fiat currency backing stablecoins is typically held by financial institutions that are either banks or third-party custodians. The choice of custodian depends on the jurisdiction and regulatory requirements for holding large fiat reserves. Reputable stablecoin issuers prefer established, regulated banks to store reserves, enhancing user trust.

Segregated Accounts: Stablecoin issuers often use segregated or dedicated accounts for holding fiat reserves to ensure that funds are isolated from the issuer's operational finances. This segregation limits risk by ensuring user funds are safeguarded and not mixed with the issuer's capital, making them theoretically protected from the issuer's financial issues, like insolvency.

Reserve Management and Composition:

Composition of Reserves: The reserve may consist of cash, cash-equivalent assets (such as short-term U.S. Treasury bonds), and sometimes other highly liquid, low-risk assets to help mitigate inflation and maintain value.

Liquidity Management: To ensure liquidity for redemption requests, reserves need to be accessible and sufficiently liquid. This means that even though some reserves may be held in assets, these assets are often short-term and easy to convert into cash if needed. The average maturity duration of these assets is kept short, typically a few months, to minimize market risk and maintain high liquidity.

Transparency and Auditing:

Proof of Reserve: Stablecoin issuers provide periodic transparency reports or proof-of-reserve verifications to assure users and regulators that the required amount of fiat is in reserve. Some issuers, such as Circle[76] (for USDC), use independent third-party accounting firms to perform regular audits or attestations to verify that reserves match or exceed the number of stablecoins in circulation.

Public Reporting Standards: Stablecoin issuers publish regular reports detailing reserve composition, often monthly or quarterly, to provide insights into the asset types backing the stablecoins and ensure compliance with financial transparency standards. These reports typically cover cash held, government securities, and other liquid assets, detailing the proportion of each asset type within the reserve.

Minting and Burning Mechanisms for Supply Management:

Minting: When a user or institution deposits fiat currency with the stablecoin issuer, a corresponding amount of stablecoin is minted (in DeFi, "mint" refers to the process of creating new tokens or assets, through a smart contract, often by locking collateral). Minting is usually conducted through centralized systems that automate the creation of stablecoins upon confirmation of fiat deposits. This process is programmed and strictly controlled to ensure the minting only occurs when the exact fiat amount has been received.

Burning (Destruction): During redemption, users return their stablecoins to the issuer, triggering the "burning" of stablecoins. Burning is a process where the stablecoins are permanently removed from circulation, managed via smart contracts. This ensures that the total supply of stablecoins decreases in line with the fiat outflow, thus maintaining the 1:1 backing ratio.

Monitoring Supply and Demand: Stablecoin issuers constantly monitor the supply and demand for their coins and adjust their minting and burning procedures accordingly. This helps maintain liquidity in the market while ensuring that they do not over-issue stablecoins, which would violate the peg.

Technology and Security Protocols:

Smart Contract Governance: The "minting" and "burning" of stablecoins are sometimes governed by smart contracts, which provide an added

---

[76] https://www.circle.com/topic/usdc

layer of transparency and security. These contracts can be audited by third-party firms to ensure they operate as expected. This approach minimizes human intervention in the issuance and destruction of tokens, reducing the risk of error or fraud.

Risk Management for Custody: Reserves are subject to risk management measures to protect against unauthorized access and hacking threats. Secure custody solutions involve multi-signature wallets and partnerships with financial institutions or custodians specializing in digital assets.

Insurance Coverage: Some stablecoin issuers secure insurance policies on fiat reserves, offering additional protection in case of security breaches or other financial risks. This insurance may cover a portion of the reserves and is typically held with reputable insurance providers to ensure financial backing.

Crypto-Collateralized Stablecoins

Crypto-collateralized stablecoins are a type of cryptocurrency-backed asset designed to maintain a stable value by using other cryptocurrencies as collateral. Unlike fiat-collateralized stablecoins, which are backed by traditional currency, these stablecoins rely on digital assets, such as Ethereum (ETH), as their reserve. Due to the inherent volatility of cryptocurrencies, crypto-collateralized stablecoins are usually over-collateralized, meaning that the collateral value exceeds the value of stablecoins issued. Here's a comprehensive look at how they operate:

Over-Collateralization and Its Purpose

Volatility Management: Cryptocurrencies are known for their price volatility, which means their market value can fluctuate significantly over short periods. Over-collateralization helps mitigate this risk. By requiring collateral that exceeds the stablecoin's value, the system can absorb price drops in the collateralized cryptocurrency without immediately risking the stablecoin's value.

Collateralization Ratios: To secure the stability of the stablecoin, users are required to maintain a specific collateralization ratio (usually 150%)

or higher. This means that for every 1 unit of stablecoin issued, the user must lock in at least 1.5 units (or more) of value in collateral. The collateral ratio can vary based on the algorithm protocol and risk associated with the underlying assets.

Automatic Liquidation: If the value of the collateral drops below the required collateralization ratio, the smart contract can trigger an automatic liquidation. This involves selling off part of the collateral to ensure the system remains fully collateralized and stable, preventing under-collateralization and protecting the value of issued stablecoins.

Examples of Crypto-Collateralized Stablecoins

sUSD by Synthetix: This is another crypto-collateralized stablecoin primarily backed by Ethereum (ETH) and SNX (Synthetix Network Token) within the Synthetix protocol. sUSD leverages over-collateralization and staking incentives to maintain its value relative to the U.S. dollar. Liquity USD (LUSD): Backed by Ethereum (ETH), LUSD is minted by depositing ETH into the "Liquity protocol", requiring a minimum collateralization ratio to ensure stability. Another example of a crypto-collateralized stablecoin is Djed[77], developed on the Cardano blockchain[78]. Djed maintains its peg to the U.S. dollar by utilizing a combination of smart contracts and over-collateralization with cryptocurrencies.

Issuance and Redemption Process via Smart Contracts

Issuance (Minting): To issue or "mint" a crypto-collateralized stablecoin, a user must lock an amount of cryptocurrency (such as ETH) in a smart contract. The value of this collateral must be higher than the stablecoins they want to create. For instance, if a user wants to mint 100 DAI, they may need to lock up $150 worth of ETH as collateral, meeting the 150% collateralization ratio.

Redemption: When users want to retrieve their locked collateral, they return the stablecoins (such as DAI) to the smart contract and "burn" them (destroying the tokens). The contract then releases the equivalent

---

[77] https://djed.xyz/restricted/?countryname=dW5pdGVkJTIwc3RhdGVz
[78] https://cardano.org

cryptocurrency collateral back to the user, if the collateralization ratio is still sufficient.

Smart Contract Automation: These issuance and redemption processes are automated through smart contracts, which are self-executing contracts with terms directly written into code on the blockchain. This decentralizes the process, eliminating the need for intermediaries and ensuring that collateralization requirements are strictly adhered to.

Collateral Management and Stability Mechanisms

Dynamic Collateralization Ratios: Some platforms adjust collateralization ratios dynamically based on the "volatility" and "liquidity" of the collateral. More volatile assets may require higher collateral ratios, ensuring stability even in highly unpredictable market conditions.

Stability Fees: To maintain the stablecoin's peg, protocols may charge a "stability fee" or interest on the collateral. This fee incentivizes users to keep their loans well-collateralized and aligns with market conditions. Stability fees are paid when users close their positions and retrieve their collateral, adding an economic layer to stabilize the system.

Collateral Vaults and Debt Positions: When users lock up cryptocurrency to mint stablecoins, they create a "collateral vault" or "collateralized debt position" (CDP). These vaults (In DeFi a "vault" refers to a smart contract that autonomously manages and optimizes users' assets according to predefined strategies) are individually managed within the protocol and can be tracked on-chain. Each vault must maintain the minimum collateral ratio; otherwise, it risks liquidation.

Liquidation Process

Automatic Liquidation: If the collateral's value falls and breaches the minimum collateralization ratio (e.g., 150%), the protocol triggers an automatic liquidation. This means the smart contract will sell or auction off part of the collateral to cover the shortfall and restore the minimum collateral level.

Auction Mechanism: In some systems, liquidated collateral is sold in an auction format where other participants can bid on it. This process helps ensure the protocol recovers sufficient value from the collateral while maintaining liquidity and fair price discovery.

Penalty Fees: To discourage users from allowing their collateral ratios to fall too low, some protocols impose penalty fees during liquidations. These fees further incentivize users to maintain their collateralization ratios above the "minimum threshold".

Decentralized Governance and Stability Mechanisms

Decentralized Governance: In decentralized protocols, stability parameters, including collateral types, collateral ratios, and stability fees, are determined by a decentralized community of token holders. These governance mechanisms allow the protocol to adapt to changing market conditions and user needs while preserving the stablecoin's peg.

Multi-Collateral Support: Some crypto-collateralized stablecoins, support multiple types of collateral beyond Ethereum. This diversified collateral pool can include various digital assets, helping to spread risk and reduce dependency on a single asset's volatility.

Peg Stabilization Mechanisms: If a crypto-collateralized stablecoin deviates from its target peg, some protocols may adjust stability fees, adjust collateralization ratios, or incentivize arbitrage opportunities to bring the stablecoin back to its intended value.

Technical and Security Considerations

Smart Contract Security Audits: Given the complex nature of these systems, the smart contracts managing crypto-collateralized stablecoins undergo regular audits by security firms. "CertiK[79]" utilizes formal verification and AI-driven analysis to provide security assessments for blockchain protocols. "OpenZeppelin[80]" offers security audits and develops open-source frameworks to enhance the safety of smart contracts. "Quantstamp[81]" provides scalable security-audit solutions for

---

[79] https://www.certik.com/products/smart-contract-audit
[80] https://www.openzeppelin.com/security-audits

blockchain applications, aiming to secure smart contracts and digital assets.

Oracle Integration: The value of the collateral is updated through oracles, which are data feeds that provide real-time price information from external sources. Oracles are essential in determining when collateralization ratios fall below the required level, triggering liquidation if necessary. Decentralized oracles are often used to avoid manipulation and increase trust in price data.

User Risk Awareness: Crypto-collateralized stablecoins expose users to price volatility risk in the collateral and liquidation risk if collateral value falls rapidly. Protocols typically include educational materials and risk disclosures to inform users about these risks before they create stablecoin positions.

Algorithmic (Non-Collateralized) Stablecoins

Algorithmic (non-collateralized) stablecoins are a unique category of stablecoins that aim to maintain a stable value without any direct physical or crypto asset backing. Instead of relying on reserves, these stablecoins utilize algorithms and smart contracts to automatically adjust their supply in response to market price fluctuations, working to keep the stablecoin's price pegged to a target value (typically $1).

Supply and Demand Adjustment Mechanism

Algorithmic Rebalancing: Algorithmic stablecoins use a supply-and-demand adjustment mechanism controlled by algorithmic rules encoded in smart contracts. When the stablecoin's price rises above its target peg (for example, $1), the algorithm increases the total supply by minting more coins, diluting the existing supply and encouraging the price to fall back to the target level. Conversely, if the price falls below the peg, the algorithm reduces the supply by burning (destroying) some coins, decreasing the total supply to increase the price.

Elastic Supply Model: This mechanism creates an "elastic" supply model, meaning that the supply of the stablecoin can expand or contract

---

[81] https://quantstamp.com/audits

automatically to maintain stability. Unlike traditional currencies or collateralized stablecoins, where supply is often fixed or only loosely adjusted, algorithmic stablecoins adjust supply frequently, based on real-time market conditions.

Examples of Algorithmic Stablecoins

Ampleforth[82] (AMPL): Ampleforth's protocol uses a "rebase" mechanism to adjust the supply of AMPL daily based on its deviation from the target price. If the price is above $1, it increases the number of AMPL tokens held in each wallet (positive rebase); if below, it reduces them (negative rebase). Despite the adjustments, each token's value remains elastic, aimed at stabilizing the currency's purchasing power.

TerraUSD (UST): TerraUSD, once a algorithmic stablecoin, used a unique dual-token model involving LUNA, another asset on the Terra network. When UST's price rose above $1, LUNA was burned to mint more UST, increasing the supply. When UST fell below $1, users were incentivized to burn UST for LUNA, reducing supply and raising the price. However, TerraUSD experienced issues during a market downturn, leading to its de-pegging and collapse.

Mechanisms to Stabilize the Peg

Expansion and Contraction Cycles:

Expansion (Positive Rebase): When demand is high, and the price of the stablecoin rises above the peg, the algorithm mints additional coins and distributes them to holders. This increase in supply dilutes the value, aiming to push the price back down toward the peg.

Contraction (Negative Rebase): When demand decreases and the price falls below the peg, the algorithm initiates a supply contraction by burning tokens or reducing the token supply. This supply reduction is intended to raise the price back up to the peg.

Rebasing and Wallet Adjustments:

---

[82] https://www.gemini.com/cryptopedia/ampleforth-protocol-ampl-coin-stablecoin

In some models, like Ampleforth, the token supply in user wallets is adjusted directly during rebase events. For example, if AMPL increases in supply, the number of tokens in each holder's wallet grows proportionally, maintaining the same overall market value but redistributing based on price changes.

Dual-Token System:

Some algorithmic stablecoins, like TerraUSD, employ a dual-token system, where one token (the stablecoin) is pegged, and the other (e.g., LUNA in the case of TerraUSD) absorbs volatility. In this system, arbitrage mechanisms allow users to exchange the pegged token for the secondary token, helping to adjust supply and maintain price stability.

Smart Contracts and Automation

The entire supply adjustment process is automated through smart contracts, which are programmed to monitor the stablecoin's market price against its target peg. When the price deviates, the smart contract initiates the necessary supply adjustment, either minting or burning tokens. To track the stablecoin's real-time market price accurately, algorithmic stablecoins use oracles. Oracles are third-party data services that fetch and relay external price data to the blockchain, ensuring the protocol has up-to-date information for executing its rebalancing functions. The accuracy and reliability of these oracles are crucial for the stability of the stablecoin.

Incentive Mechanisms

Many algorithmic stablecoins provide financial incentives to encourage users to buy or sell tokens in ways that stabilize the price. For instance, when the price falls below the peg, users may be incentivized to buy the stablecoin at a discount, expecting it to return to its peg, thereby profiting from the eventual price correction.

Staking and Rewards: Some models offer rewards or staking opportunities for users who participate in the stabilization mechanism. For example, if users burn tokens during a contraction period, they may be compensated with other tokens or staking rewards to encourage participation.

Risks and Challenges of Algorithmic Stablecoins

De-Pegging and Market Dependency: Algorithmic stablecoins can be vulnerable to extreme market conditions. If demand for the stablecoin falls rapidly, the contraction mechanisms may struggle to keep pace, leading to a "death spiral," where the stablecoin de-pegs and fails to recover. TerraUSD's collapse exemplified this, as the algorithm couldn't sustain the peg in a market-wide downturn.

Reliance on Arbitrage and Market Confidence: These systems rely heavily on user confidence and the ability of arbitrage mechanisms to function effectively. If market participants lose "confidence" or if arbitrage incentives are "insufficient", the stablecoin can de-peg. This reliance on market participants' rational behavior introduces risk, as external shocks or market manipulation can disrupt stability.

Oracle and Smart Contract Risks: The stability of algorithmic stablecoins is also dependent on "accurate price data" and "secure smart contracts". Oracle failures, hacks, or errors in smart contract code could lead to incorrect supply adjustments, potentially destabilizing the peg.

Governance and Adaptability

Algorithmic stablecoins often rely on decentralized governance, where holders of governance tokens can vote on changes to parameters like expansion/contraction rates, rebase frequencies, and incentive structures. This governance flexibility allows the system to adapt to changing market conditions and make protocol adjustments that may enhance stability. To respond to the cryptocurrency market's volatile nature, some algorithmic stablecoin protocols dynamically adjust rebase[83] parameters, contraction speeds, or incentives based on broader market trends. Such adaptability can help buffer against volatility, although it may not completely mitigate risk.

---

[83] https://kauri.finance/academy/what-are-rebase-tokens

Benefits of Stablecoins

Stablecoins provide several key advantages, especially within the cryptocurrency and decentralized finance (DeFi) ecosystems, due to their unique characteristics:

Stablecoins serve as a stable store of value amid the often-volatile cryptocurrency market, making them ideal for a variety of financial transactions. They function effectively as a medium for daily transactions, savings, or even as a unit of account. For example, traders frequently convert cryptocurrencies into stablecoins such as USDC during periods of high market instability, allowing them to preserve value without converting to fiat currency.

Accessibility: Stablecoins offer a universally accessible stable currency that can be particularly advantageous in regions with unstable local currencies or limited access to traditional banking systems. This makes them an attractive option in countries experiencing economic challenges, such as hyperinflation, where people might prefer to hold stablecoins like USDT over their depreciating local currency. This accessibility extends to anyone with an internet connection, democratizing access to a stable form of money.

Efficiency in Transactions: The use of stablecoins can significantly enhance the efficiency of financial transactions, especially across borders. They facilitate fast, low-cost transfers that are particularly advantageous over traditional banking channels, which can be slow and costly. This makes stablecoins an excellent choice for remittances and general international payments. For instance, sending USDC to another country can be quicker and cheaper than using conventional wire transfer services, making it an efficient tool for global trade.

Interoperability in DeFi: In the DeFi sector, stablecoins are pivotal, often used as collateral for lending, borrowing, and executing trades. Their stability and easy integration into various DeFi protocols enhance liquidity and enable smooth financial operations across different platforms. On DeFi platforms, users can deposit stablecoins to earn interest or use them as collateral to borrow other cryptocurrency assets, leveraging their stable value for more speculative investments or additional liquidity.

Risks and Challenges

While stablecoins provide significant benefits within cryptocurrency and DeFi environments, they also face several risks and challenges that can impact their stability and reliability:

Centralization Risks: Fiat-collateralized stablecoins like USDT and USDC operate under "centralized control", relying on specific entities to manage their reserves and handle the issuance. This centralization introduces counterparty risks, where the stability and integrity of the stablecoin depend on the financial health and regulatory compliance of the central issuer. For instance, if the entity behind USDC encounters legal or financial issues, it could disrupt the redemption process and destabilize the stablecoin.

Regulatory Risks: Stablecoins, particularly those that are fiat-collateralized, often attract significant regulatory attention. Regulatory bodies may impose strict rules that could affect the operation and stability of these stablecoins. For example, regulatory measures could compel stablecoin issuers to adhere to traditional banking regulations, potentially restricting how these coins are issued or used.

Collateralization Risks: Crypto-collateralized stablecoins face risks associated with the volatility of their underlying collateral. If the market value of the collateral drops sharply, it might not sufficiently back the value of the stablecoins, leading to potential liquidations. For example, a significant drop in the price of ETH could trigger widespread liquidations of related DAI collateral, destabilizing the stablecoin's value.

Algorithmic Failure: Algorithmic stablecoins, which use a formula to manage their supply and maintain their peg to another asset, can fail if the algorithm does not function as expected. This was starkly demonstrated by the collapse of TerraUSD (UST) in May 2022, where the stablecoin rapidly lost its peg to the US dollar, resulting in severe "devaluation" and loss of user confidence.

Transparency Issues: There are ongoing concerns about the transparency regarding the reserves backing some stablecoins, especially those that are fiat collateralized ones. The lack of regular, verifiable audits raises doubts about whether these stablecoins.

Key Stablecoins in the Market

Several stablecoins have emerged as prominent players in the cryptocurrency market, each utilizing different mechanisms and targeting various use cases:

Table 11: Stablecoin Types, Peg, Use Case and Issuer comparison

Stablecoin	Type	Peg	Use Case	Issuer
Tether (USDT)	Fiat-collateralized	Pegged 1:1 to the US dollar	Used for trading, liquidity, and as a stable store of value	Issued by Tether Limited; faced scrutiny regarding reserve transparency but provides regular attestations.
USD Coin (USDC)	Fiat-collateralized	Pegged 1:1 to the US dollar	Popular in trading and DeFi; stable medium of exchange	Jointly issued by Circle and Coinbase; backed by regularly attested reserves.
DAI	Crypto-collateralized	Aims to 1:1 value with USD	Utilized in DeFi for collateral, trading, and lending	Managed by MakerDAO; decentralized and over-collateralized with crypto assets.
Binance USD (BUSD)	Fiat-collateralized	Pegged 1:1 to the US dollar	Used on Binance exchange and in DeFi	Issued by Paxos in partnership with Binance; issuance halted following regulatory

			applications	scrutiny, but existing tokens remain usable.
Pax Dollar (USDP)	Fiat-collateralized	Maintains strict 1:1 peg with the US dollar	Used in DeFi, trading platforms, and as a store of value	Issued by Paxos Trust Company; regulated by the NYDFS with transparent reserve holdings.
TrueUSD (TUSD)	Fiat-collateralized	Pegged 1:1 to the US dollar	Used in trading, DeFi, and as a stable store of value	Managed by TrustToken; backed by reserves with attestations provided by third-party accounting firms.
TerraUSD (UST) - Historical	Algorithmic (formerly)	Designed to maintain 1:1 peg with USD	Initially used for payments, trading, and in DeFi	Issued by the Terra blockchain and managed by Terraform Labs; collapsed in May 2022 due to instability in its algorithmic mechanism.

Importance of Stablecoins in the Financial Ecosystem

Stablecoins have become a fundamental component of both the cryptocurrency and traditional financial ecosystems, serving multiple crucial roles:

<u>Medium of Exchange:</u> Stablecoins facilitate trading within the cryptocurrency ecosystem by allowing traders to move in and out of volatile assets without the need to convert to fiat currency. This utility is especially valuable on cryptocurrency exchanges where stablecoins like

USDC or USDT are often used as a base currency for trading pairs, enabling smoother and more predictable transactions.

Store of Value: During periods of high market volatility, stablecoins provide a "safe haven" for investors looking to preserve the value of their assets without exiting the cryptocurrency market entirely. For instance, investors might convert volatile cryptocurrency holdings into a stablecoin such as USDT during downturns to avoid losses while maintaining liquidity.

Cross-Border Payments and Remittances: Stablecoins offer a swift and cost-effective solution for cross-border payments and remittances, circumventing the high fees and slow processing times associated with traditional banking systems. They are particularly useful for sending money to regions with unstable currencies, ensuring that the recipient receives the full value sent without losses due to currency fluctuations or banking fees.

Lending and Borrowing in DeFi: Within DeFi protocols, stablecoins are indispensable for lending and borrowing activities. They are commonly used both as collateral and as the assets lent out, providing a stable basis for these transactions. For example, users might deposit stablecoins like DAI into platforms such as Compound to earn interest or use them as collateral to borrow other cryptocurrencies.

Yield Farming and Staking: In the DeFi space, stablecoins are frequently employed in yield farming and staking strategies, where they are used to provide liquidity. Users often choose stablecoin pairs for liquidity provision to minimize risks associated with price volatility, thereby avoiding impermanent loss and generating steady returns.

On-Ramps and Off-Ramps: Acting as a bridge between the traditional financial system and the crypto markets, stablecoins simplify the process for users to enter and exit the cryptocurrency space. They allow for easy conversion from fiat currencies to crypto and vice versa, facilitating participation in various cryptocurrency activities and easing the withdrawal process to bank accounts.

The Future of Stablecoins

Regulatory Developments:

Stablecoins are attracting increasing attention from governments and regulatory bodies, suggesting that more defined regulatory frameworks are on the horizon. These regulations may cover aspects such as reserve transparency, issuance practices, and usage in financial transactions, aiming to increase the trustworthiness and strength of stablecoins. For instance, proposals in the U.S. to regulate stablecoin issuers similarly to banks could enhance the credibility and security surrounding these digital assets.

Central Bank Digital Currencies (CBDCs):

The exploration and potential rollout of Central Bank Digital Currencies (CBDCs) by various nations could significantly impact the role of private stablecoins. CBDCs are essentially "crypto-digital forms of fiat currencies" that could fulfill many of the roles currently played by stablecoins, but with complete government backing. For example, China has been advancing its "crypto-digital yuan", which could provide a state-backed alternative to privately issued stablecoins, offering similar benefits but with enhanced security and regulatory compliance.

Cross-Chain Stablecoins:

The increasing complexity of the cryptocurrency ecosystem may boost the prevalence of cross-chain stablecoins, which can operate across multiple blockchain platforms. This would enable more fluid and versatile use of stablecoins across diverse networks, enhancing their utility in DeFi and broader crypto applications. An example of this trend is USDC's expansion across blockchains like Ethereum, Solana, and Algorand, which broadens its usability and accessibility.

Algorithmic Stability Innovations:

Despite some high-profile failures, the development of algorithmic stablecoins is likely to continue, with efforts focusing on creating more sophisticated models that maintain stability without traditional collateral. These innovations might include advanced economic models or hybrid systems that blend various mechanisms to ensure price stability more effectively.

Integration with Traditional Finance:

There is potential for deeper integration of stablecoins within the traditional financial sector. Stablecoins could increasingly be used for settlements, payments, and value transfers among financial institutions. For example, banks might start offering accounts based on stablecoins or incorporate these digital assets into their payment systems to facilitate faster and more cost-effective transactions. In 2023, the Office of the Comptroller of the Currency[84] (OCC) authorized nationally chartered banks to use stablecoins for payment activities, enabling faster and more cost-effective transactions. Also, JPMorgan have developed their own stablecoins, such as JPM Coin[85], to facilitate seamless interbank transfers and settlements.

Stablecoins serve as critical bridges between traditional finance and the expanding DeFi space, providing stability, efficiency, and accessibility in an extremely volatile market. As regulatory frameworks evolve and technology advances, stablecoins are poised to play an increasingly significant role in global finance, potentially transforming how value is transferred and stored across the world.

---

[84] https://www.occ.gov/news-issuances/news-releases/2021/nr-occ-2021-2.html
[85] https://www.jpmorgan.com/onyx/documents/deposit-tokens.pdf

Yield Farming

Yield farming is a decentralized finance (DeFi) strategy where cryptocurrency holders earn rewards by lending or staking their assets in liquidity pools on DeFi platforms. Essentially, yield farming allows users to generate "passive income" by providing liquidity to DEXs or lending protocols. The process involves depositing cryptocurrencies into smart contracts, which aggregate funds into pools that facilitate trading or lending, while generating fees. In return for contributing to these pools, users receive rewards, often paid in the "platform's native tokens", which can be reinvested for compounding returns. Yield farming strategies vary widely, ranging from stablecoin pools to more volatile pools with higher reward potential, often involving complex multi-step processes like borrowing, lending, and reinvesting across multiple protocols to maximize returns. The yields are dynamic, influenced by market demand, the pool's liquidity, and the protocol's incentive structure. While yield farming can offer extreme returns, it carries risks, including smart contract vulnerabilities, impermanent loss, and potential volatility in token values, requiring participants to manage these risks actively.

Details of yield farming

Yield farming, often referred to as "liquidity mining", is a DeFi strategy that allows cryptocurrency holders to earn rewards by depositing their assets into liquidity pools on DeFi platforms. In this context, users who contribute assets to these pools are known as liquidity providers (LPs). By participating in yield farming, LPs support the liquidity and functionality of DeFi protocols, which rely on user-supplied funds for various financial services like lending, borrowing, and decentralized exchanges (DEXs). In return for their contributions, LPs earn rewards, which can include transaction fees, interest on loans, or additional tokens provided by the platform, often as part of an incentive structure.

Yield farming is the practice of lending or staking cryptocurrency assets in exchange for rewards. The assets are deposited into liquidity pools, which are essentially smart contracts that aggregate user funds to provide liquidity for DeFi protocols. These liquidity pools are crucial for decentralized exchanges and lending platforms, as they enable the smooth operation of DeFi transactions without relying on centralized intermediaries. In return for contributing their funds, LPs earn various types of rewards, including:

Transaction Fees: A portion of the fees generated from transactions within the liquidity pool is distributed to LPs based on their share of the pool.

Interest Payments: For lending-based platforms, LPs can earn interest on their deposits, as their funds are loaned out to borrowers on the platform.

Additional Tokens or Governance Tokens: Many DeFi platforms offer governance tokens (such as Compound's COMP or Uniswap's UNI) as an incentive to LPs. These tokens can either be sold or used within the platform to vote on protocol decisions.

How Yield Farming Works: The Role of Liquidity Pools

Yield farming primarily takes place within liquidity pools. A liquidity pool is a "smart contract that holds funds", enabling trading, lending, and borrowing on a DeFi platform. Each liquidity pool pairs two or more tokens (e.g., ETH and USDC) to facilitate decentralized trading without a traditional order book. Here's how it works:

Depositing Assets: To start yield farming, a user must deposit cryptocurrencies into a liquidity pool. For example, on Uniswap, a user might deposit equal values of ETH and USDC to create a trading pair.

Earning Returns: Once deposited, the user's assets are available for use in the pool. Traders can exchange between the paired tokens, or the assets can be loaned out to borrowers. In return, the LP earns a portion of the trading fees or interest paid by borrowers.

Incentives in Governance Tokens: Some DeFi platforms further incentivize LPs by rewarding them with governance tokens. These tokens can often be staked, sold, or used to participate in protocol governance.

Yield farming typically involves the following steps

The process of liquidity provision and earning rewards typically unfolds on decentralized finance (DeFi) platforms:

Deposit/Provide Liquidity: Users begin by depositing a specific pair of cryptocurrencies into a liquidity pool on a DeFi platform. These platforms use liquidity pools to facilitate decentralized trading, lending, and other financial services..

Receive Liquidity Provider (LP) Tokens: In exchange for adding liquidity to the pool, users receive "LP tokens". For instance, on "SushiSwap", users who contribute assets to a liquidity pool receive SushiSwap Liquidity Provider (SLP) tokens. These tokens represent the user's share of the pool and can be used or "staked" (to earn interest) to participate further in the DeFi ecosystem. These tokens are a way for users to reclaim their share of the liquidity pool later, along with any rewards accrued from transactions made through the pool.

Earn Rewards: Participation in liquidity pools can be rewarding. Rewards typically come in several forms:

> Transaction Fees: Users earn a portion of the transaction fees generated from trades that utilize the liquidity pool.

> Interest: On platforms where pools are used for lending, liquidity providers can earn interest from borrowers who use the pool's assets.

> Governance Tokens: Some platforms incentivize liquidity providers by issuing governance tokens, such as UNI on Uniswap or SUSHI[86] on SushiSwap, which can also be traded or used to participate in protocol governance.

Staking (Optional): Liquidity providers may also stake their LP tokens on the same platform or others to earn additional rewards. This is often

---

[86]https://stormgain.com/blog/uniswap-uni-vs-sushiswap-sushi-whats-difference

referred to as "yield farming", where staked LP tokens generate further earnings, typically in the form of "additional tokens" from the platform.

Withdrawal: Users can decide to withdraw their contribution from the liquidity pool at any time. Upon doing so, they can reclaim the original tokens they deposited, plus any rewards earned during the period of their investment. This makes liquidity pools flexible and relatively liquid investment options within the DeFi. By engaging in these activities, users not only contribute to the liquidity and functionality of DeFi platforms but also have the opportunity to earn "passive income" through several reward mechanisms.

Types of Yield Farming Strategies

Yield farming strategies in DeFi exhibit a broad range of complexity and risk levels, supplying to different investor profiles and risk appetites:

Simple Liquidity Provision: This is the most straightforward form of yield farming, where users simply provide liquidity to a DeFi liquidity pool and earn returns primarily from transaction fees generated by the trading activity within that pool. Some pools also distribute governance tokens as additional rewards, which can increase the profitability of the investment.

> Example: A user might deposit DAI and ETH into a liquidity pool on Uniswap and earn a share of the transaction fees whenever someone trades between these two assets.

Staking LP Tokens: After participating in a liquidity pool, users receive liquidity provider (LP) tokens that represent their stake in the pool. These LP tokens can then be staked in other DeFi protocols, which may offer additional rewards in the form of other tokens or higher yield rates.

> Example: A user could take LP tokens received from Uniswap and stake them in a protocol like SushiSwap to earn SUSHI tokens.

Leveraged Yield Farming: For those seeking higher returns and willing to take on greater risk, leveraged yield farming involves borrowing assets to increase the scale of liquidity provided. This approach amplifies both potential returns and potential risks, as it involves exposure to market volatility and the risk of liquidation if asset values fluctuate significantly.

> Example: Using borrowed DAI from a lending platform such as Aave to provide additional liquidity in a opportunity on another platform could significantly increase potential returns and risks.

Cross-Platform Farming: This strategy involves moving assets across various platforms to capitalize on the best available yields and bonuses offered by different DeFi protocols. It requires active management and understanding of multiple platforms to optimize returns effectively.

> Example: A user might deposit collateral on Compound, borrow against it, and then use those borrowed funds to engage in yield farming on another DeFi platform like "Yearn.finance[87]" or "Balancer[88]".

Benefits of Yield Farming

Yield farming offers several significant advantages for users interested in leveraging their cryptocurrency holdings to earn passive income. Here's a detailed look at some of the key benefits:

Yield farming can provide exceptionally high returns, especially compared to traditional financial investments. This is particularly true in liquidity pools that are in high demand or during periods of peak activity in the DeFi market, where APRs can be triple digits. This potential for high yields is driven by the dynamic and often volatile nature of the DeFi ecosystem, where "token economics" can greatly reward early and active participants.

Many DeFi platforms incentivize participation by distributing their native governance tokens to liquidity providers and yield farmers. These tokens can sometimes accrue substantial value and offer additional earnings on top of the regular interest or fee shares from providing liquidity. For example, platforms like Compound distribute "COMP

---

[87] https://yearn.fi
[88] https://balancer.fi

tokens" to users who lend or borrow on the platform, providing a secondary stream of income that can significantly enhance overall yields.

Earning governance tokens not only has financial benefits but also allows token holders to participate in the "governance of DeFi protocols". This participatory role includes voting on important decisions such as protocol upgrades, changes to system parameters, or even directing the future development paths of the platforms. Holding UNI tokens (This token is an Ethereum-based that facilitates the Uniswap protocol, a decentralized exchange utilizing an automated market maker) model to enable seamless swapping of ERC-20 tokens, for instance, enables users to vote on various governance proposals on Uniswap, directly influencing the protocol's operation and evolution.

Yield farming plays a critical role in fostering the growth and enhancing the liquidity of DeFi protocols. By locking in funds, yield farmers help to ensure that there is enough capital flowing through these systems to support trading, lending, and other financial services, making them more robust and efficient. This contribution is fundamental for maintaining the strength and competitiveness of the DeFi ecosystem, encouraging further innovation and adoption.

Risks and Challenges

While yield farming can offer substantial rewards, it also exposes participants to significant risks that must be carefully managed:

Impermanent Loss: This risk occurs when the prices of tokens in a liquidity pool diverge significantly from when they were deposited. If one asset in a paired liquidity pool, like an ETH/USDT pool, appreciates rapidly, the liquidity provider may suffer an impermanent loss. This means they could end up with less of the appreciated asset than if they had simply held the tokens outside of the pool, despite earning trading fees.

Smart Contract Risk: Yield farming operations depend on the integrity and security of smart contracts. These contracts can contain bugs or vulnerabilities that might be exploited by attackers, leading to the loss of funds. An example of this risk materialized when a DeFi protocol's smart contract was exploited, resulting in significant losses for liquidity providers.

Liquidity Risk: In some cases, especially in smaller or less popular pools, there might not be enough liquidity to allow for easy withdrawal of one's assets without affecting the prices of the tokens in the pool. If a provider tries to withdraw a large stake from such a pool, it could lead to high slippage and financial loss.

Volatility and Market Risk: The cryptocurrency market is volatile, which can substantially impact the assets used in yield farming. A sharp decline in the price of tokens being farmed or those used as collateral in farming can lead to significant losses, potentially wiping out any gains from transaction fees or other rewards.

Popular Yield Farming Platforms

Several platforms have emerged as key players in the yield farming landscape, each offering unique opportunities and features tailored to different strategies and goals in DeFi:

Uniswap enable users to provide liquidity to various trading pairs. Liquidity providers earn trading fees generated from the swaps that occur in their pool. Additionally, Uniswap distributes its governance token, UNI, to liquidity providers as an incentive, which can also be used in protocol governance. Users can provide liquidity to pairs like ETH/USDC and earn a share of the trading fees along with potential UNI token rewards.

"SushiSwap", initially forked from "Uniswap", enhances the typical decentralized exchange model by offering additional incentives. It provides SUSHI tokens to liquidity providers who stake their liquidity provider (LP) tokens. SUSHI tokens not only serve as a reward but also confer governance rights within the SushiSwap ecosystem. By providing liquidity and staking LP tokens in SushiSwap, users can earn SUSHI tokens in addition to transaction fees.

"Yearn.finance" acts as a yield aggregator that automates the process of moving user funds between different DeFi protocols to maximize returns. This platform is known for its innovative strategies that dynamically shift assets to the most profitable yield farming opportunities available at any given time. Users deposit funds into "Yearn's vaults[89]", which then automatically handle the strategies to optimize the yields from various other DeFi platforms.

"Compound" is a decentralized lending platform where users can lend their cryptocurrencies and earn interest on them. Additionally, the platform distributes its COMP governance tokens to both lenders and borrowers, which can be used to participate in the governance of the protocol. Lending assets like DAI or USDC on Compound allows users to earn interest on their deposits and accumulate COMP tokens as additional rewards.

Aave offers a lending and borrowing protocol that supports a range of activities including traditional yield farming. Users can earn interest on their deposits and potential AAVE tokens[90] as rewards. Aave also supports innovative products like flash loans[91], which allow for unique leveraged yield farming strategies. Depositing assets into Aave not only generates interest but also possibly earns AAVE tokens, enhancing the overall yield.

The Future of Yield Farming

As the DeFi landscape matures, several trends are likely to shape the evolution of yield farming, making it more sophisticated and potentially expanding its appeal:

Improved Risk Management

The DeFi ecosystem is expected to develop enhanced tools for assessing and managing risks associated with yield farming. Innovations like impermanent loss calculators and more demanding smart contract audits[92]

---

[89] https://yearn.fi/vaults
[90] https://aave.com
[91] https://aave.com/docs/developers/flash-loans
[92] https://hacken.io/services/dapp-audit/

"dapps" are likely to become standard, helping participants better understand and mitigate risks. This improvement in risk management tools will make yield farming more secure and accessible, attracting a broader base of users.

Cross-Chain Yield Farming

The interconnection of different blockchains through technologies like blockchain bridges and interoperability protocols is set to enable cross-chain yield farming. This would allow users to seamlessly farm yields across multiple networks.

Institutional Participation

As DeFi protocols become more robust and regulatory frameworks more defined, institutional investors are expected to enter the yield farming space. This influx of institutional money could bring substantial liquidity, although it may also lead to more competitive yields. Institutional participation would not only validate the sector but could also drive innovations and adoption of best practices in risk management and transparency.

Governance Tokens

Governance tokens are a fundamental aspect of DeFi platforms, enabling a democratic mechanism through which token holders can influence the direction and operations of a project. These tokens empower their holders with the right to propose, vote on, and implement changes to the platform, reflecting a shift from traditional centralized control to a more community-driven governance structure.

Key Features of Governance Tokens:

Decision-Making Power: Holders of governance tokens have the authority to participate in decision-making processes that affect the platform's future. This can include changes to protocols, fee structures, product features, and more.

Proposing Changes: Token holders can propose changes or new features. Proposals that meet certain criteria (often requiring a minimum number of tokens to initiate) can be put forward for community voting.

Voting Rights: Governance tokens grant holders the right to vote on proposals. The influence of a voter may depend on the number of tokens held, aligning the voting power with the stake in the platform.

Examples of Governance Tokens:

COMP token holders can propose and vote on protocol upgrades and changes within the "Compound" finance ecosystem. This could include adjustments to the interest rate models or changes to the types of collateral accepted by the platform.

UNI tokens allow holders to vote on key governance decisions, such as the usage of the protocol's treasury funds, changes to transaction fee structures, or updates to the protocol itself.

The distribution and use of governance tokens can significantly impact the autonomy and evolution of a DeFi platform. They are designed to incentivize users who are actively involved in the ecosystem and to align their interests with the long-term success of the platform. This model not only promotes transparency and community involvement but also helps ensure that the platform remains adaptable and responsive to its users' needs.

How Governance Tokens Work

Governance tokens allowing stakeholders to participate actively in managing and evolving the protocol. Here's a closer look at how governance tokens are used within these platforms:

Proposal Creation: Holders of governance tokens have the capability to propose changes to the platform. This democratic feature empowers users to suggest enhancements ranging from minor adjustments to significant protocol overhauls.

> Example: A COMP token holder might propose modifications to the interest rate model on the Compound platform to make it more competitive or fair.

Voting Process: Token holders participate in the governance process by voting on proposals. Each token generally represents one vote, although some platforms might use mechanisms like "quadratic voting" to balance influence more equitably among holders, preventing those with large holdings from having overwhelming control.

> Example: On Uniswap, when a proposal to alter the fee structure is introduced, all UNI token holders can cast their votes based on the number of tokens they hold. The decision to implement the change depends on the majority vote or other specific quorum requirements set by the protocol.

Proposal Execution: If a proposal is approved based on the voting results, it is executed automatically through the platform's smart contracts. This automation ensures that the changes are implemented swiftly and accurately without manual intervention.

> Example: For platforms like Aave, if a proposal to modify borrowing rates achieves the necessary votes, the smart contract

system automatically adjusts the rates according to the new parameters voted on.

This system not only fosters a high degree of transparency and community involvement but also aligns the interests of the users with the long-term strength and evolution of the DeFi platform.

Distribution of Governance Tokens

Governance tokens distribution plays a crucial role in engaging community involvement and aligning user interests with the platform's development. Here's an overview of the common distribution strategies:

Initial Distribution: Governance tokens can be initially distributed through various methods such as "token sales", "airdrops", or "direct issuance". These approaches are aimed at incentivizing early adopters, developers, and other key stakeholders who contribute to the platform's early development and growth.

> Example: Uniswap famously distributed UNI tokens via an airdrop (an "airdrop" refers to the distribution of free tokens or cryptocurrencies to users' wallets, typically as a promotional strategy to raise awareness and encourage adoption of a new project) to users who had interacted with the platform prior to a specific date, rewarding those who helped to establish and grow the Uniswap ecosystem.

Ongoing Distribution: Many DeFi protocols incentivize ongoing participation and engagement by distributing governance tokens as rewards. This can include activities like "providing liquidity", "staking", or simply using the "platform's services". The idea is to continually reward users for their contributions to the protocol's condition and liquidity.

> Example: "Compound" rewards its users with COMP tokens for both supplying and borrowing assets on the platform. The distribution rate is proportional to the user's level of interaction and the amount of transaction fees they generate.

Liquidity Mining: This is a popular method to distribute tokens, where users earn governance tokens in exchange for providing liquidity to the platform's pools. This strategy not only rewards users but also secures essential liquidity for the platform's operation, helping to stabilize and enhance the platform's functionality.

> Example: "SushiSwap" offers SUSHI tokens to users who provide liquidity to its various trading pairs. This approach not only rewards users but also ensures there is sufficient liquidity to facilitate trading on the platform.

These distribution mechanisms are designed to foster a robust and active community, crucial for the decentralized decision-making process integral to DeFi platforms.

Benefits of Governance Tokens

Governance tokens are instrumental in decentralized ecosystems, offering multiple advantages that enhance the operation and community engagement of DeFi platforms:

Decentralization: Governance tokens are pivotal for decentralizing decision-making within blockchain projects. By distributing governance powers across a broad user base, these tokens reduce the dependency on any central authority, ensuring that the platform remains resistant to censorship and centralized control issues.

> Example: In MakerDAO, holders of the MKR token have the power to vote on crucial protocol decisions, such as the inclusion of new collateral types and adjustments to DAI's stability fee. This process confirms that decisions are made by those who are actively invested in the protocol's success.

Incentivizing Participation: Governance tokens serve as a strong incentive for users to engage with the platform actively. By rewarding users with tokens for activities like "liquidity provision", "staking", or "governance participation", platforms encourage ongoing contribution, which is essential for their sustainability.

> Example: "Curve Finance" rewards its users with CRV tokens for providing liquidity. These tokens not only represent a financial stake but also grant voting rights in protocol governance, thereby incentivizing users to contribute to and maintain the platform's liquidity pools.

Alignment of Interests: Distributing governance tokens aligns the interests of users with the long-term success of the platform. As token holders gain the right to vote on proposals that affect the platform's future, they are likely to support decisions that enhance the platform's value and their potential returns.

> Example: UNI token holders are motivated to vote for enhancements and updates that increase Uniswap's overall utility and market position, boosting the underlying value of both the platform and the UNI token itself.

Creation of Community: Governance tokens are critical in fostering a strong community ethos among platform users. This community-driven approach not only promotes active participation but also empowers users to take part in the platform's development.

> Example: Aave's community, guided by AAVE token governance, is active in governance forums, discussing and voting on proposals that impact the protocol's direction and implementation.

Risks and Challenges of Governance Tokens

While governance tokens in DeFi platforms enhance community engagement and "democratize decision-making", they also introduce several risks and challenges that could impact the effectiveness and fairness of the governance model:

Concentration of Power: A significant risk with governance tokens is the potential concentration of voting power among a few large holders or entities. This centralization can undermine the decentralized ethos of DeFi by allowing major stakeholders to influence governance decisions disproportionately, potentially leading to decisions that favor a minority at the expense of the broader community.

> Example: If a small number of investors or entities accumulate a large portion of governance tokens, they could influence significant changes or veto proposals against the community consensus, potentially skewing development in their favor.

Low Participation Rates: Often, only a small fraction of governance token holders actively participates in governance processes. This low participation rate can result in decisions that do not necessarily reflect the broader community's preferences or best interests.

> Example: In many DeFi protocols, governance decisions can be dominated by a limited group of participants due to general apathy or disinterest from the majority of token holders, leading to a lack of diverse input and potentially skewed governance outcomes.

Voter Apathy: Voter apathy is prevalent among token holders who may be more interested in the speculative aspects of token ownership rather than the governance of the platform. This disengagement can lead to a lack of informed decision-making and reduce the effectiveness of the governance process.

> Example: Token holders who acquire governance tokens for speculative purposes may not participate in voting, resulting in a lower turnout and decisions being made by a small, perhaps less representative, group of voters.

Potential for Manipulation: The governance model can be susceptible to manipulation by coordinated groups who accumulate enough tokens to influence governance decisions. This could lead to proposals that undermine the protocol's security, benefit certain groups disproportionately, or alter the protocol in harmful ways.

> Example: Colluding actors could manipulate governance decisions to initiate protocol changes that facilitate unfavorable

actions, such as draining pooled funds or altering the protocol's rules to their advantage.

The Role of Governance Tokens in DeFi

Governance tokens continue to play a crucial role in the evolution of decentralized finance (DeFi) platforms, embodying principles that promote user participation and community-driven development.

Empowering Users Governance tokens empower users by giving them a voice in significant decisions that shape the platforms they utilize. This empowerment is crucial for maintaining the decentralized ethos of DeFi, ensuring that no single party can unilaterally control the protocol. This democratization of financial systems enables a broader base of users to influence how the protocols are managed and developed.

"Enhancing Community Engagement" by allowing token holders to vote on proposals that affect the platform, governance tokens foster a deeper sense of community and commitment among users. This engagement helps ensure that the platform evolves in response to the collective input and consensus of its user base, rather than the vision of a centralized team. The active participation of community members in governance processes helps sustain long-term interest and loyalty, strengthening the overall health of the platform.

Growth Governance tokens contribute to the sustainability and growth of DeFi protocols by aligning the interests of the users with those of the platform. When users have a stake in the decision-making process, they are more likely to contribute positively and help drive the platform towards success.

Governance tokens are a catalyst for innovation within DeFi protocols. They allow users to propose and vote on new features, integrations, and changes, ensuring that the platform remains at the forefront of technological advancement. The ability to adapt and innovate based on community feedback is vital for DeFi platforms as they navigate the highly competitive and rapidly evolving blockchain ecosystem.

While governance tokens provide numerous benefits, they also present challenges such as potential centralization if a few large holders accumulate significant voting power. Furthermore, low voter turnout can lead to decisions that do not reflect the broader community's desires. DeFi projects must therefore continually refine their governance models to ensure fairness, representativeness, and active participation.

Future Developments in Governance Tokens

As the DeFi ecosystem matures, the role and mechanisms of governance tokens are poised to evolve significantly. Here are some expected trends and developments:

Improved Governance Mechanisms: DeFi may see the adoption of more advanced and equitable voting systems such as quadratic voting. This method curtails the disproportionate influence of large token holders by escalating the cost of additional votes, making governance more democratic.

> Example: A protocol could implement quadratic voting to balance the voting power between large and small token holders, ensuring that the governance process reflects a broader community consensus.

Interoperability of Governance Tokens: With the growing interconnectivity between different blockchain platforms, governance tokens might become interoperable, allowing token holders to participate in governance activities across various blockchains.

> Example: A governance token issued on Ethereum could also allow holders to participate in governance decisions on protocols operating on other blockchains like Polkadot or Binance Smart Chain.

Enhanced Incentives for Participation: To combat low participation rates in governance activities, protocols may offer additional incentives for active participation, such as bonus tokens or other rewards.

> Example: Protocols could reward participants with additional governance tokens or fee discounts for consistently voting on proposals or participating in governance discussions.

DAO-Driven Innovation: Decentralized Autonomous Organizations (DAOs) will likely play an increasingly central role in project governance, including the allocation of funds for new initiatives or partnerships.

> Example: A DeFi protocol managed by a DAO could use its governance tokens to vote on funding new platform features or integrating new technologies.

Regulatory Considerations: As regulatory scrutiny of DeFi increases, governance tokens may need to incorporate mechanisms to comply with legal standards, potentially including identity verification processes for token holders.

> Example: Protocols might require KYC verification for governance participants, especially for votes that involve significant financial decisions or changes to the protocol's financial structure.

As DeFi platforms develop and interface more with traditional financial systems, governance tokens could influence decisions on hybrid platforms that merge decentralized technologies with traditional financial operations.

Interoperability

Interoperability in the context of blockchain and DeFi refers to the ability of different blockchain networks and their associated protocols to communicate, share information, and execute transactions across multiple blockchains seamlessly. Interoperability is a critical aspect of the broader adoption and effectiveness of blockchain technology, as it enables various blockchain networks to work together.

Interoperability in blockchain is the capability of different blockchain networks to interact with each other. This interaction can involve "transferring assets", "sharing data", or "executing smart contracts" across different chains without the need for intermediaries. The goal is to create a more connected and efficient blockchain ecosystem where users and developers can leverage the strengths of multiple networks.

Why is Interoperability Important?

Different blockchains can specialize in specific functions. For instance, one blockchain may handle transactions with exceptional speed, while another may be optimized for executing complex smart contracts. Interoperability allows these specialized systems to work together seamlessly, enhancing overall network efficiency.

With interoperability, users can enjoy a smoother experience when interacting with multiple blockchain systems. It simplifies processes such as token transfers between different ecosystems, reducing the need for multiple wallets and streamlining the user's interaction with diverse blockchain applications.

By allowing data and assets to move freely between disparate blockchains, interoperability enables the development of new applications that leverage the strengths of various networks. For example, Wrapped Bitcoin (WBTC) enables Bitcoin holders to access Ethereum's DeFi ecosystem. By tokenizing Bitcoin as an ERC-20 asset, WBTC allows users to leverage Bitcoin's liquidity while utilizing Ethereum's smart contract functionalities in decentralized applications.

Interoperability can significantly enhance liquidity within the DeFi ecosystem. It allows for the pooling of resources across different platforms, making assets more readily available for various uses. This not only increases the capital efficiency of the assets themselves but also broadens the scope and functionality of DeFi applications, making them more powerful and versatile.

How Interoperability Works

Interoperability between different blockchain networks can be achieved through several mechanisms, each designed to facilitate seamless exchanges of information and value across diverse blockchain systems. Here's how these approaches work:

Cross-Chain Bridges: Cross-chain bridges connect two different blockchains, enabling the transfer of assets and data between them. This mechanism helps to overcome the isolationist nature of many blockchains.

> Example: Wrapped Bitcoin (WBTC) on the Ethereum blockchain allows Bitcoin holders to use their BTC within Ethereum's ecosystem, particularly in DeFi applications.

Sidechains: Sidechains are separate blockchains that run parallel to a primary blockchain, connected by a two-way peg. (A two-way peg is a mechanism that allows assets to move seamlessly between a primary blockchain and its sidechain at a fixed or predetermined exchange rate. This ensures that assets transferred to the sidechain can be returned to the primary blockchain with equivalent value, enabling interoperability and consistent value representation across both networks). They can operate under different rulesets and feature sets, tailored to specific use cases like faster transactions or enhanced privacy.

> Example: Polygon (formerly Matic Network) functions as a sidechain to Ethereum, helping to offload transactions from the main Ethereum chain to improve scalability and reduce costs.

Interoperability Protocols: These protocols create a framework that enables different blockchains to interact and communicate with each other. They often provide a standardized way of exchanging data and executing transactions across networks.

> Example: Cosmos and Polkadot facilitate not just the transfer of tokens but also a range of interactions between different blockchains, promoting a more integrated network of blockchains.

Atomic Swaps: Atomic swaps allow for the exchange of cryptocurrencies from different blockchains directly between parties, without the need for intermediaries like exchanges. They use smart contracts to ensure that transactions either succeed or fail on both sides.

> Example: Direct swaps between cryptocurrencies such as Bitcoin and Litecoin, enabling users to trade one for the other without third-party intermediation.

Interchain Communication: This involves direct communication protocols between blockchains, allowing them to share data and value without the need for bridging technology.

> Example: The Inter-Blockchain Communication (IBC) protocol in the Cosmos ecosystem facilitates secure and trustless interactions between independent blockchains, enabling the seamless transfer of assets and data across various networks. IBC protocol enables transaction and information flows across connected blockchains, facilitating functional multi-chain ecosystem.

Key Projects and Protocols Promoting Interoperability

Several blockchain projects are leading the charge in promoting interoperability among different blockchain networks, each bringing unique technologies:

Cosmos: Often described as the "Internet of Blockchains," Cosmos is designed to facilitate an ecosystem of blockchains that can interact and scale efficiently.

Technology: It utilizes the Tendermint consensus[93] mechanism and the Inter-Blockchain Communication (IBC) protocol to enable seamless interactions between its network of blockchains.

Use Cases: This setup allows projects built on Cosmos to transfer data and assets fluidly across various blockchains, enhancing functionality and user experience across its ecosystem.

Polkadot: This platform provides a multi-chain framework that allows various blockchains (parachains[94]) to operate independently yet securely interoperate through a shared relay chain.

Technology: It uses a central relay chain for security and interoperability, enabling "parachains" to process transactions in parallel and exchange data with strong security guarantees.

Use Cases: By facilitating cross-chain transfers of data and assets, Polkadot supports a diverse range of applications, from financial services to novel data services.

Wanchain[95]: This platform aims to build a distributed financial infrastructure that enables private, cross-chain interactions.

Technology: It leverages secure multiparty computation and custom cross-chain communication protocols, focusing on connecting and exchanging value between different blockchains.

Use Cases: Particularly focused on enabling DeFi applications, Wanchain supports cross-chain functionality, allowing for decentralized exchange of assets across disparate networks.

Chainlink: Primarily known as a decentralized oracle network, Chainlink (CCIP) also contributes significantly to blockchain interoperability[96] by

---

[93]https://docs.tendermint.com/v0.34/introduction/what-is-tendermint.html
[94] https://kusama.network/parachains/
[95] https://www.wanchain.org

facilitating reliable data feeds to smart contracts on various networks. CCIP stands out as the sole interoperability protocol offering Level 5 security. In cross-chain blockchain systems, Level 5 security, referred to as "Defense-In-Depth," signifies the highest level of protection. This method leverages multiple decentralized networks to secure each cross-chain transaction, ensuring enhanced decentralization and robust resilience.

>Technology: Chainlink nodes operate as oracles that provide external data (e.g., weather, prices) to smart contracts, bridging the gap between blockchains and real-world data.

>Use Cases: It supports complex smart contracts and extends the functionality of blockchains by allowing access to real-time data feeds, web APIs, and traditional bank payments.

Benefits of Interoperability

Interoperability in blockchain technology enhances the functionality of blockchain networks by enabling them to complement each other's strengths. For instance, one blockchain could focus on processing transactions swiftly while another ensures robust security. This interoperability increases liquidity, allowing assets to flow freely across different blockchains and improving the effectiveness of DeFi platforms where liquidity is crucial.

The ability to connect unequal blockchain systems reduces the overall fragmentation of the crypto ecosystem. This connection leads to a more cohesive environment where data and digital assets can be utilized across various platforms without the barriers that typically segment networks.

From a user perspective, interoperability leads to a smoother experience. It allows users to interact with multiple blockchains seamlessly, without the need to switch between different platforms or manage multiple wallets. This ease of use is critical for wider adoption and user satisfaction.

---

[96] https://chain.link/cross-chain

Additionally, interoperability fosters innovation by giving developers the freedom to build applications that leverage the best features of multiple blockchains. This integration can lead to new use cases and rapid advancements in blockchain technology, pushing the industry toward more comprehensive and sophisticated solutions.

Overall, the push towards interoperable blockchain networks is likely to make blockchain technology more accessible, powerful, and user-friendly, paving the way for more integrated and efficient solutions within the ecosystem.

Challenges and Risks of Interoperability

Interoperability in blockchain technology, while highly beneficial, introduces various challenges:

Security Risks: The interconnection of different blockchains increases the complexity of security, expanding the potential attack surface. Notably, cross-chain bridges, which facilitate the transfer of assets between blockchains, have been prone to attacks. In 2021, Poly Network, a cross-chain DeFi platform, suffered a security breach in which attackers exploited vulnerabilities to transfer digital assets to their own wallets. This occurred due to a vulnerability in the protocol's smart contract, specifically within the function responsible for "verifying cross-chain" transactions.

Complexity: Achieving seamless interoperability is technically challenging. Ensuring that different blockchain networks can communicate efficiently, without errors or inconsistencies, requires sophisticated integration solutions and constant maintenance.

Standardization Issues: Interoperability is hindered by the lack of standardized protocols across different blockchains. Each blockchain may operate under different standards, making it difficult to ensure smooth interaction between them. Efforts to standardize blockchain protocols are crucial but complex, involving coordination across multiple stakeholders.

Governance and Consensus: Coordinating governance across different blockchain platforms can be complicated. Discrepancies in how networks should interact or integrate can lead to disagreements within and between different blockchain communities, potentially stalling interoperability initiatives.

Scalability Concerns: As blockchains become interconnected, the volume of transactions crossing these networks can increase significantly, posing scalability challenges. Ensuring that blockchain infrastructures can handle a higher volume of cross-chain transactions without compromising performance is essential.

Future of Interoperability

Interoperability is playing a transformative role in the evolution of blockchain technology, driving a series of significant trends and developments:

The enhancement of interoperability protocols will likely lead to the multiplying of cross-chain DeFi ecosystems. This will allow for more fluid movement of assets and liquidity across different blockchain platforms, enabling users to utilize decentralized finance applications that draw on resources from multiple blockchains.

The concept of a global network of blockchains that can interact seamlessly with each other is gradually becoming more realistic. Such development would facilitate a decentralized internet of blockchains, enhancing efficiency and connectivity across various platforms and applications.

Just as the early internet saw the establishment of fundamental protocols and standards, the blockchain space may develop its own set of interoperability standards. These standards would promote uniformity and facilitate easier integration across different blockchain systems, potentially accelerating widespread adoption.

Enhanced interoperability could encourage more collaboration between various blockchain projects. As projects align their efforts to develop compatible technologies, the pace of innovation and the breadth of new applications are likely to increase.

As regulatory landscapes evolve, interoperability might play a crucial role in enabling compliance across different jurisdictions. This could be particularly beneficial for integrating blockchain technology with traditional financial systems, aiding in its broader acceptance and use.

New Trends in DeFi

Interoperability is increasingly recognized as a crucial element for the next phase of blockchain development. It enhances the ability of different blockchain networks to work together, share resources, and broaden the range of potential applications. Here are some emerging trends in decentralized finance (DeFi) that are expected to shape its future:

Perpetual Liquidity Pools (PLPs)[97] offer continuous liquidity for various assets, enabling trading without expiration dates. This approach increases efficiency, reduces slippage, and can potentially offer higher yields. Intents-Based Architecture[98] simplifies DeFi interactions by allowing users to express their financial goals, and then automatically executing the necessary actions to achieve those goals. This reduces complexity and improves the overall user experience.

Points and Airdrop Meta[99] involve platforms rewarding users with points or tokens for various activities. These can be redeemed for rewards or used in governance decisions, which encourages community engagement, promotes platform adoption, and creates a gamified experience. Liquid Staking Protocols[100] allow users to stake their crypto assets without locking them up, thereby maintaining liquidity. This increases capital efficiency, allows for participation in multiple DeFi protocols simultaneously, and generates additional yield.

---

[97] https://bitcoinworld.co.in/exploring-perpetual-liquidity-pools-the-future-of-decentralized-finance/
[98] https://www.paradigm.xyz/2023/06/intents
[99] https://www.coinbase.com/learn/crypto-basics/understanding-the-new-meta-of-crypto-points-farming
[100] https://www.kucoin.com/learn/crypto/top-liquid-restaking-protocols

Decentralized Asset Management Platforms[101] provide automated investment strategies, yield optimization, and portfolio management tools. They democratize access to sophisticated financial management, reduce costs, and enhance transparency. These trends reflect the ongoing evolution of the DeFi landscape, offering exciting possibilities for both users and developers. As the industry matures, we can expect to see further innovative solutions that enhance the functionality and accessibility of decentralized financial services.

---

[101] https://www.lcx.com/introduction-to-decentralized-asset-management/

DeFi and Traditional Investment

This chapter examines how DeFi platforms compare to traditional investment frameworks across various categories. The focus is on fixed income, stock dividends, real assets, real estates, savings accounts, synthetic assets and decentralized derivatives, REITs, and Certificate of Deposits. Each subdivision explores the key aspects of risk profile, return on investment, liquidity, complexity, and regulatory and security considerations. Through this comparison, the chapter provides insights into how DeFi platforms differ from and interact with conventional financial systems, highlighting their implications for investors.

DeFi and Fixed Income Securities

Fixed income securities, such as bonds, are traditionally seen as safer investments compared to the volatile world of DeFi.

Risk Profile

Bonds, particularly government bonds, are considered low-risk investments. The primary risk associated with bonds is credit risk (the risk that the issuer will default), interest rate risk, and inflation risk.

DeFi: DeFi platforms carry significantly higher risks, including smart contract risks, impermanent loss, market volatility, and regulatory risks. The yields can be higher, but so are the potential losses.

Return on Investment

Bonds typically offer lower returns compared to DeFi. Government bonds might yield 4% annually (November 27, 2024, the yield on a 10-year U.S. Treasury bond was approximately 4.25%), while corporate bonds can offer slightly higher returns depending on the credit rating of the issuer.

DeFi: Yields in DeFi can be much higher, often ranging from 5% to over 100% annually, depending on the platform, the assets involved, and the current market conditions. As of December 1, 2024, various platforms offer competitive interest rates on stablecoins and cryptocurrencies. Notably, "Notional" provides the highest stablecoin yield, offering up to 18.17% on USDC. For cryptocurrencies, "Nexo" offers up to 15% on

"Polkadot" (DOT)[102]. These rates are subject to change and may come with specific terms and conditions. However, these high returns come with substantial risk.

Liquidity

Bonds are generally less liquid than DeFi assets. Selling a bond before its maturity date can result in a loss if market conditions have changed. However, many bonds are traded on secondary markets, providing some liquidity.

DeFi: DeFi assets can be very liquid, especially in high-volume platforms. However, liquidity can dry up quickly during market downturns, and there is always the risk of slippage or inability to withdraw during peak times.

Complexity

Bonds are relatively straightforward financial instruments. Investors buy bonds, earn interest (coupon payments), and receive their principal back at maturity.

DeFi can be complex, with various platforms offering different yield farming strategies, liquidity pools, staking options, and governance mechanisms. Understanding these mechanisms is essential to managing risk and optimizing returns.

Regulation and Security

Bonds are heavily regulated, especially government bonds. Investors have legal protections, and the risk of fraud is minimal.

DeFi operates in a largely unregulated space, which can expose investors to fraud, hacks, and other risks without legal recourse.

---

[102] https://bravenewcoin.com/insights/best-crypto-interest-rates

Table 12: Comparative Analysis of Traditional Bonds vs. DeFi

Feature	Bonds	DeFi
Risk Profile	Low-risk (credit, interest rate, inflation)	High-risk (smart contract, impermanent loss, market volatility, regulatory)
Return on Investment	Lower (1-4% for government bonds)	Higher (5-100%+)
Liquidity	Moderate (secondary market)	High (in stable conditions)
Complexity	Relatively simple	Complex (various strategies, mechanisms)
Regulation and Security	Heavily regulated, low fraud risk	Largely unregulated, higher fraud risk

DeFi and Stock Dividend Returns

While DeFi yield farming and stock dividends both offer returns on investment, they are fundamentally different in terms of risk profile, return potential, and the mechanisms by which returns are generated.

Risk Profile

DeFi yield farming is generally much riskier than investing in dividend-paying stocks. The risks include smart contract vulnerabilities, impermanent loss, market volatility, and regulatory uncertainty. Additionally, the nascent and rapidly evolving nature of DeFi means that the risk of platform failures or exploits is higher.

Stocks: Dividend-paying stocks are generally considered lower risk, particularly if the company has a strong track record of stable earnings and dividend payments. The primary risks include market risk, company-specific risk (such as business performance), and economic downturns, which can lead to reduced dividends or stock price declines.

Return on Investment

DeFi yield returns can be extremely high, sometimes reaching triple digits annually, particularly when platforms offer additional incentives like governance tokens. However, these high returns are accompanied by significant risks.

Dividend yields are typically lower, with most dividend-paying stocks offering yields in the range of 2% to 5% annually. However, these returns are generally more stable and predictable, especially with established companies.

Liquidity

Liquidity in DeFi can vary significantly depending on the platform and the assets involved. In times of market stress, liquidity can dry up quickly, making it difficult to exit positions without significant slippage.

Stocks, particularly those of large, established companies, are usually very liquid, meaning they can be bought and sold easily without significantly affecting the price. However, selling stocks during a market downturn can still result in losses.

Complexity

DeFi: Yield farming in DeFi can be complex, requiring a deep understanding of the underlying smart contracts, the platform's risk factors, and the specific mechanisms by which yields are generated. Users also need to actively manage their positions to optimize returns and mitigate risks.

Stocks: Investing in dividend-paying stocks is generally straightforward. Investors buy shares and receive dividends based on the number of shares held. There is less need for active management, although monitoring the company's financial health is still important.

Regulatory and Legal Framework

DeFi operates in a largely unregulated environment, which contributes to the higher risk but also the potential for higher returns. However, the lack of regulation means there is little recourse if things go wrong, such as in cases of fraud or platform failure. DeFi platforms are increasingly required to implement Anti-Money Laundering "AML" and Know Your Customer "KYC" protocols to prevent illicit activities. The Financial Action Task Force (FATF) has recommended that virtual asset service providers adhere to these standards, ensuring that DeFi platforms collect and verify user identities to mitigate money laundering[103].

---

[103]https://www.fatf-gafi.org/en/publications/fatfrecommendations/

Stocks are heavily regulated, and investors benefit from protections such as those provided by the Securities and Exchange Commission (SEC) in the United States. Companies are required to disclose financial information, and investors have legal avenues to pursue in cases of fraud or malpractice[104].

Table 13: Comparing the DeFi and dividend-paying stocks

Aspect	Defi	Stocks
Risk Profile	High Risk: Vulnerabilities, Impermanent Loss, Volatility, Regulatory Uncertainty	Lower Risk: Market Risks, Company-Specific Risks, Economic Downturns
Return On Investment	Very High Potential Returns (Up to Triple Digits), With High Risk	Lower, Stable Returns (2-5% Annually)
Liquidity	Variable, Can Dry Up Quickly in Market Stress	High, Especially for Large, Established Companies
Complexity	Complex: Requires Understanding of Contracts, Active Management	Simpler: Passive Income Through Dividends, Less Active Management Needed
Regulatory Framework	Largely Unregulated, Higher Risk of Fraud, Little Recourse in Disputes	Heavily Regulated, Protections from Entities Like the SEC, Recourse Available in Disputes

DeFi and Real Asset Returns (Gold and Silver)

Real assets like gold and silver have long been considered safe-haven investments, offering a different risk and return profile compared to DeFi yield farming.

Risk Profile

DeFi yield farming is generally high-risk due to the potential for smart contract failures, impermanent loss, market volatility, and regulatory uncertainty. These platforms are part of a nascent, rapidly evolving ecosystem, which adds to the risk.

Gold and silver are considered low-risk investments, especially during times of economic uncertainty. They are tangible assets with intrinsic value and have historically served as a hedge against inflation and

---

documents/guidance-rba-virtual-assets.html
[104]https://www.sec.gov/rules-regulations/statutesregulations

currency devaluation. However, they are not without risk, as their prices can be affected by market demand, interest rates, and geopolitical events.

Return on Investment

Yields in DeFi can be extremely high, sometimes reaching triple-digit percentages annually, especially when platforms offer additional incentives like governance tokens. However, these high returns come with significant risk.

Returns on gold and silver are typically lower and more stable. These assets appreciate over time, but the returns are usually in the single-digit percentages annually. The primary benefit of investing in gold and silver is wealth preservation rather than high returns.

Liquidity

Liquidity in DeFi can vary significantly depending on the platform and the assets involved. While some assets can be highly liquid, others may suffer from low liquidity, especially during market downturns.

Gold and silver are highly liquid assets, easily traded on global markets. Physical gold and silver can be sold quickly at market value, and their market depth ensures that large transactions can be executed without significantly affecting the price.

Complexity

Yield farming in DeFi is complex and requires a deep understanding of the underlying mechanisms, risks, and strategies involved. Active management is often necessary to optimize returns and manage risks effectively.

Investing in gold and silver is relatively straightforward. Investors can buy physical bullion, invest in ETFs that track the price of gold or silver, or buy shares in mining companies. The complexity is minimal compared to DeFi, and the need for active management is low.

Regulatory and Legal Framework

DeFi operates in a largely unregulated space, which can lead to significant risks. There is little legal recourse in cases of fraud or platform failures, and the regulatory environment is uncertain.

Gold and silver are well-regulated assets, with established markets and legal protections for investors. The trading of these assets is governed by international laws, and there are clear legal frameworks for ownership and transactions.

Table 14: DeFi yield farming and investing in gold and silver

Aspect	DeFi	Gold/Silver
Risk Profile	High-risk: Potential for smart contract failures, impermanent loss, volatility, regulatory uncertainty	Low risk: Market demand, interest rates, geopolitical events can affect prices
Return on Investment	Very high potential returns (up to triple digits annually), with significant risk	Lower, stable returns; primarily for wealth preservation, with single-digit percentage growth
Liquidity	Variable; highly liquid in some cases, low liquidity during downturns	High liquidity: easily traded globally, large transactions do not significantly affect prices
Complexity	Complex: Requires deep understanding and active management	Straightforward: Options include physical assets, ETFs, or shares in mining companies
Regulatory Framework	Largely unregulated, high risk of fraud, little legal recourse, uncertain regulatory environment	Well-regulated, established legal protections, governed by international laws

DeFi yield and Real Estate Returns

Real estate has long been considered a stable and reliable investment, offering a different risk-return profile compared to DeFi yield farming. Here's how they compare:

Risk Profile

DeFi yield farming is generally high-risk due to the potential for smart contract failures and platform attacks, impermanent loss, market volatility, and regulatory uncertainty. The risks associated with DeFi are often higher due to the nascent and rapidly evolving nature of the crypto ecosystem. Real estate is generally considered a lower-risk investment, particularly in stable markets. The primary risks in real estate include market fluctuations, interest rate changes, property-specific risks (such as maintenance costs), and location-related risks. Real estate values tend to be more stable over time.

Return on Investment

DeFi yields can be extremely high, especially when platforms offer additional incentives. However, these high returns come with significant risk and are often unsustainable in the long term. Real estate typically offers steady returns through rental income and property appreciation. Annual returns from rental income usually range from 4% to 10%, depending on the location, property type, and market conditions. Additionally, property values often appreciate over time, contributing to overall returns.

Liquidity

Liquidity in DeFi can vary depending on the platform and the crypto assets involved. While some assets are highly liquid, others may suffer from low liquidity, especially during market downturns. DeFi assets can typically be liquidated quickly, though not always at favorable prices. Real estate is generally considered illiquid compared to financial assets like stocks or DeFi tokens. Selling a property can take weeks or months, depending on market conditions. However, real estate investments are often viewed as long-term, reducing the need for immediate liquidity.

Complexity

Yield farming in DeFi is complicated and requires a deep understanding of the instruments, risks, and strategies. Active management is often necessary to optimize returns and manage risks effectively. Real estate investing is relatively straightforward but requires knowledge of the property market, property management, and financing options. While less complex than DeFi, real estate investing still involves significant due diligence and ongoing management.

Regulatory and Legal Framework

DeFi operates in a unregulated space, which can lead to significant risks. There is little legal recourse in cases of fraud, platform failures, or other issues. The regulatory environment is uncertain, and changes could impact DeFi platforms' operations. Real estate is a highly regulated asset class with established legal frameworks governing transactions, ownership rights, and tenant-landlord relationships. Investors benefit from clear legal protections and can enforce their rights in court if necessary.

Table 15: DeFi yield farming and real estate investing

Aspect	Defi	Real Estate
Risk Profile	High-Risk: Smart Contract Failures, Impermanent Loss, Market Volatility, Regulatory Uncertainty	Lower-Risk: Market Fluctuations, Interest Rate Changes, Property-Specific and Location Risks
Return On Investment	Extremely High Potential Returns with Significant Risk	Steady Returns Through Rental Income (4%-8% Annually) And Property Appreciation
Liquidity	Variable; Can Be Highly Liquid or Suffer from Low Liquidity During Downturns	Generally Illiquid; Selling Can Take Weeks or Months
Complexity	Complex: Requires Deep Understanding of Mechanisms, Risks, And Active Management	Moderately Complex: Needs Knowledge of Market, Management, And Financing
Regulatory Framework	Largely Unregulated, High Risk of Fraud, Uncertain Regulatory Environment	Highly Regulated with Established Legal Frameworks, Clear Legal Protections

DeFi Platforms and Savings Accounts

Savings accounts offered by traditional banks provide a very different risk-return profile compared to DeFi platforms. Here's a detailed comparison:

Risk Profile

DeFi platforms carry significant risks, including smart contract vulnerabilities, market volatility, impermanent loss, and regulatory uncertainty. These risks can lead to the loss of some or all the invested funds.

- Savings accounts are low-risk investments, typically insured by government agencies such as the FDIC in the United States. The primary risks are low returns and potential inflation risk, where the return on savings might not keep up with the rate of inflation.

Return on Investment

Yields on DeFi platforms can be much higher (near %18 APY on some platforms), depending on the platform, the assets involved, and market conditions. However, these high returns are accompanied by risks.

- Savings accounts generally offer low returns, typically around 0.01% to 1% annually, depending on the bank and the type of account. Some high-yield savings accounts provide annual percentage yields (APYs) near or above 5.00%. While these returns are guaranteed, they are significantly lower than those offered by DeFi platforms.

Liquidity

While some assets can be liquidated quickly, others may suffer from low liquidity, especially during market downturns. Additionally, transaction fees on the blockchain (such as gas fees on Ethereum) can be high, affecting net returns.

- Savings accounts offer high liquidity, allowing account holders to withdraw their funds at any time without penalty (except in the case of some specific types of accounts like certificates of deposit). However, transaction limits might apply to certain types of accounts.

Complexity

Using DeFi platforms requiring knowledge of cryptocurrency, blockchain technology, and the specific DeFi platform's mechanisms. Active management is often necessary to optimize returns and manage risks.

- Savings accounts are straightforward and require little to no management. Funds deposited in a savings account accrue interest over time, with no need for active involvement by the account holder.

Regulatory and Legal Framework

DeFi operates in generally unregulated environment, which can lead to legal uncertainties and lack of protections. Users must rely on the integrity of the platform and the security of the underlying smart contracts and blockchain.

- Savings accounts are heavily regulated by government entities, offering a high level of protection for depositors. In the U.S., for example, savings accounts are insured up to $250,000 per depositor by the FDIC, providing peace of mind and security[105].

Table 16: DeFi platforms and savings accounts

Aspect	Defi Platforms	Savings Accounts
Risk Profile	High Risk: Smart Contract Vulnerabilities, Market Volatility, Impermanent Loss, Regulatory Uncertainty	Low Risk: Insured By Agencies Like The FDIC, Low Returns, Potential Inflation Risk
Return On Investment	High Potential Returns But with High Risks	Low Returns (0.01% To 1% Annually), But Guaranteed and Stable
Liquidity	Variable Liquidity: Transaction Fees Can Impact Net Returns	High Liquidity: Easy Access to Funds, Though Transaction Limits May Apply

---

[105] https://www.fdic.gov/resources/deposit-insurance/understanding-deposit-insurance

Complexity	Complex: Requires Understanding of Cryptocurrencies, Blockchain, And Defi Mechanics	Straightforward: Minimal Management Required, Simple Interest Accrual
Regulatory Framework	Largely Unregulated, Which Increases Risks and Legal Uncertainties	Heavily Regulated with Strong Protections for Depositors, Such as FDIC Insurance In The U.S.

Synthetic Assets and Decentralized Derivatives

Synthetic assets and decentralized derivatives are specialized financial instruments in the DeFi space that allow users to gain exposure to traditional assets or complex financial products without holding the underlying assets. They are often used for hedging, speculation, and gaining exposure to assets that are otherwise difficult to access within the crypto ecosystem.

Synthetic Assets and Decentralized Derivatives instruments are also accessible to crypto users but require a deeper understanding of financial markets and derivative products. Synthetic assets and derivatives are used for specialized financial strategies, including hedging against price movements, gaining exposure to non-crypto assets, and leveraging trades.

Risk Profile

High risk due to potential vulnerabilities in blockchain and smart contracts. Exploits or bugs can lead to significant financial losses. High volatility can impact returns, particularly in yield farming and liquidity provision, where the value of assets can fluctuate dramatically.

Synthetic Assets and Decentralized Derivatives: Despite being decentralized, there is still counterparty risk, particularly related to the collateral backing synthetic assets or the liquidity of derivatives. Decentralized derivatives often involve leverage, which amplifies both potential gains and losses, making them higher risk than typical DeFi activities.

Return on Investment

Returns are linked to trading volume and liquidity, offering potentially stable returns in high-volume pools.

- Synthetic Assets and Decentralized Derivatives: Synthetic assets and derivatives can offer significant speculative returns, particularly in volatile markets. However, the use of leverage increases the risk. These instruments are also used for hedging and arbitrage, which can provide lower but more stable returns compared to outright speculation.

Complexity

DeFi platforms can be complicated, but many are designed to be user-friendly. Understanding specific platform mechanics, such as yield farming or liquidity provision, is necessary to optimize returns.

- Synthetic Assets and Decentralized Derivatives: These instruments are more complex and require a deep understanding of financial derivatives, market dynamics, and the specific risks associated with synthetic assets or leveraged products.

Liquidity

Generally sufficient liquidity, especially on well-established platforms like Uniswap or Aave. However, liquidity can be an issue during market downturns or on smaller platforms.

- Synthetic Assets and Decentralized Derivatives: Liquidity can vary significantly depending on the platform and the specific synthetic asset or derivative. Liquidity may be lower for more complex or niche products, leading to difficulty in closing positions.

Regulatory and Legal Framework

DeFi is largely unregulated, which allows for innovation but also introduces legal uncertainties. There is a risk that future regulations could impact platform operations or user access.

Synthetic assets and decentralized derivatives, which replicate traditional financial instruments like stocks or commodities, are increasingly subject to regulatory scrutiny due to their resemblance to conventional securities and commodities.

Table 17: DeFi platforms and synthetic assets

Aspect	DeFi Platforms	Synthetic Assets and Decentralized Derivatives
Risk Profile	Smart Contract Risks: High risk from vulnerabilities. Market Volatility: High volatility impacts return.	Counterparty Risk: Risks linked to collateral and liquidity. Leverage Risk: High risk from potential amplified losses.
Return on Investment	Yield Farming and Staking: High returns exceeding 100% APY but significant risks. Trading Fees: Linked to trading volume, potentially stable.	Speculative Returns: High potential in volatile markets. Hedging/Arbitrage: Lower, more stable returns.
Complexity	Moderate but varies; understanding of platform mechanics necessary.	High; requires deep knowledge of financial derivatives and market dynamics.
Liquidity	Varies by platform and market conditions.	Variable, often lower for complex or niche products, which may cause slippage.
Regulatory and Legal Framework	Largely unregulated, posing legal uncertainties and potential future regulation impacts.	Likely higher regulatory scrutiny, legal risks if classified under securities laws.

DeFi Platforms and REITs

DeFi platforms and Real Estate Investment Trusts (REITs) are both investment vehicles that offer potential returns, but they operate in vastly different markets with distinct risk-return profiles.

Market Risk

The cryptocurrency market is highly volatile, with prices of digital assets often experiencing large swings. This volatility affects the value of assets on DeFi platforms, impacting returns from activities like yield farming or liquidity provision.

Real Estate Market Fluctuations: REITs are subject to market risk tied to the real estate sector. Factors such as interest rates, economic conditions, and property values can impact REIT performance. However, real estate markets are generally less volatile than cryptocurrencies. REITs may also face risks related to specific properties, such as vacancy rates, lease defaults, or property damage. Example: During economic downturns, commercial REITs might see reduced occupancy rates, impacting rental income and dividends.

Liquidity Risk

High transaction fees (especially on Ethereum) and periods of network congestion can reduce liquidity. Additionally, liquidity may dry up quickly during market downturns. Example: During a sharp market decline, users might find it difficult to withdraw liquidity from pools without incurring significant losses.

Publicly traded REITs are typically highly liquid, as they are traded on major stock exchanges. Investors can buy or sell shares relatively easily, similar to trading stocks. Private REITs, on the other hand, are less liquid, and investors may face restrictions on when and how they can redeem their shares. Example: An investor in a publicly traded REIT can quickly sell shares during market hours, but an investor in a private REIT might have to wait for a redemption window.

Regulatory Risk

This lack of oversight introduces significant legal risks, including the potential for fraud, lack of consumer protections, and the possibility of sudden regulatory crackdowns that could impact platform operations. If a government imposes strict regulations on DeFi platforms, users might face restrictions or lose access to their funds.

REITs are subject to stringent regulations, particularly in the U.S., where they must comply with specific rules under the Internal Revenue Code (IRC) to qualify as a REIT. This includes distributing at least 90% of taxable income as dividends to shareholders[106]. Investor Protections: The regulation of REITs provides investors with a higher level of security and transparency, including regular financial disclosures and protections

---

[106] https://www.irs.gov/instructions/i1120rei?utm_source

under securities laws. Example: REIT investors benefit from clear legal protections and regular income distributions, which are required by law.

Complexity

Participating in DeFi platforms requires a good understanding of blockchain technology, cryptocurrency markets, and the specific DeFi protocols in use. Activities like yield farming and liquidity provision can be complex and require active management. Example: A user providing liquidity on "Uniswap" must understand the risks of impermanent loss, how to manage gas fees, and how the AMM (automated market maker) model works.

Investing in REITs is relatively straightforward, especially with publicly traded REITs. Investors buy shares in a REIT, similar to buying stocks, and receive dividends based on the REIT's income from real estate investments. An investor in a REIT like "Realty Income" simply buys shares and receives monthly dividend payments without needing to manage the underlying real estate.

Security Risks

DeFi platforms are targets for hackers due to the large amounts of funds they handle and the decentralized nature of the ecosystem. A security breach can lead to significant financial losses for users. In 2021, the "Poly Network", a DeFi platform, suffered a security breach in which attackers exploited a vulnerability in its smart contracts, resulting in the unauthorized transfer of over $610 million in digital assets[107] to addresses controlled by the hackers. REITs face security risks related to the physical assets they own, such as damage from natural disasters.

Return on Investment

Many DeFi platforms reward users with governance tokens, which can increase in value over time, adding to the overall return. Yield farming on a platform like SushiSwap might yield high returns due to both trading fees and additional rewards in the form of SUSHI tokens. REITs

---

[107]https://www.forbes.com/sites/jonathanponciano/2021/08/10/more-than-600-million-stolen-in-ethereum-and-other-cryptocurrencies-marking-one-of-cryptos-biggest-hacks-ever/

typically provide steady, reliable income through dividends, which are often higher than the yields on traditional bonds or savings accounts. Dividend yields on REITs generally range from 1% to 8% annualized forward dividend yield[108]. In addition to dividends, REIT investors can also benefit from capital appreciation if the value of the properties owned by the REIT increases over time. A REIT like Prologis "PLD" (pays quarterly dividend) may offer a 3-4% dividend yield, with the potential for additional returns through the appreciation of its industrial real estate portfolio.

Diversification

DeFi platforms offer diversification opportunities within the cryptocurrency ecosystem, allowing investors to spread their investments across different tokens, platforms, and strategies. However, this diversification is still within a highly volatile asset class. Example: An investor might diversify their DeFi portfolio by providing liquidity on Uniswap, lending on Aave, and staking tokens on Ethereum 2.0. REITs offer diversification within the real estate sector, across different types of properties (e.g., residential, commercial, industrial) and geographic locations. Investing in a REIT index fund can further enhance diversification across multiple REITs.

Tax Considerations

DeFi Platforms:
The tax implications of DeFi activities can be complex, particularly in jurisdictions where cryptocurrency transactions are taxable events. Users may face taxes on both capital gains and income generated from activities like yield farming. Example: An investor earning interest from lending on Aave may need to report the earnings as income, and any sale of governance tokens for fiat might trigger capital gains taxes.

REIT dividends are typically taxed as ordinary income, but there are tax advantages such as the 20% qualified business income (QBI) deduction available for REIT dividends in the U.S. REITs are also required to distribute most of their income, making them tax efficient.

---

[108]https://www.dividend.com/reit-industry-dividend-stocks-etfs-and-funds/

Table 18: DeFi platforms and Real Estate Investment Trusts (REITs)

Aspect	DeFi Platforms	REITs
Market Risk	High volatility, smart contract vulnerabilities, potential for significant losses. Example: Harvest Finance exploit.	Less volatile, risks tied to real estate market dynamics and specific property issues. Example: Reduced occupancy rates during downturns.
Liquidity Risk	Variable liquidity, high transaction fees can impact returns. Example: Slippage during market downturns.	High liquidity in public REITs, less in private REITs. Example: Easy trading of public REIT shares vs. redemption restrictions in private REITs.
Regulatory Risk	Largely unregulated, potential for sudden legal impacts. Example: Possible future government crackdowns.	Heavily regulated, offers more legal protections. Example: Regular financial disclosures required.
Complexity	Requires deep understanding of blockchain and DeFi protocols. Example: Managing impermanent loss on Uniswap.	Relatively straightforward, passive management. Example: Buying shares in a REIT like Realty Income.
Security Risks	High due to hacker targets and decentralized nature. Example: Poly Network hack.	Risks mostly physical, less prone to cyber threats. Example: Property damage from natural disasters.
Return on Investment	Potentially very high but volatile APYs, rewards in governance tokens. Example: High APYs on SushiSwap.	Steady income through dividends, potential capital appreciation. Example: Dividend yield plus value increase in Prologis properties.
Diversification	Within the crypto ecosystem, still subject to high volatility. Example: Diversifying	Across different property types and regions, lower overall volatility. Example: Simon

	across various DeFi protocols.	Property Group's diversified real estate portfolio.
Tax Considerations	Complex implications, taxes on capital gains and DeFi income. Example: Taxes on Aave lending income and governance token sales.	Tax advantages for dividends, requirements to distribute most income. Example: Benefits from QBI deduction in the U.S.

DeFi Yields and Certificates of Deposit (CDs)

DeFi platforms and Certificates of Deposit (CDs) are investment instruments that offer returns, but they cater to different types of investors and come with distinct risk-return profiles. Comparison of the risks and returns associated with DeFi platforms and CDs:

Risks

DeFi platforms operate without traditional intermediaries, utilizing smart contracts to automate transactions. Examples: Aave, Compound, and Uniswap are well-known DeFi platforms that allow users to earn interest, trade tokens, or provide liquidity in exchange for fees and rewards.

CDs are time deposits offered by banks and credit unions that provide a fixed interest rate in exchange for locking up a deposit for a predetermined period. CDs are considered low-risk investments, with the return determined by the term length and the interest rate offered at the time of purchase. CDs can be offered with various terms, typically ranging from a few months to several years, with longer-term CDs generally offering higher interest rates.

Market Risk

DeFi platforms are closely tied to the cryptocurrency market, which is highly volatile. The value of assets on these platforms can fluctuate significantly, affecting the returns from activities like yield farming, staking, or liquidity provision. Exploits or failures in t smart contracts can result in significant financial losses.

CDs are considered low-risk investments because they are not exposed to market volatility. The principal amount is secure, and the interest rate is fixed for the duration of the CD term. Interest Rate Risk: While CDs are low risk, they are subject to interest rate risk. If interest rates rise after you lock in a CD, you could miss out on higher returns available elsewhere. Example: If you invest in a 5-year CD at a 2% interest rate and rates rise to 3% after your purchase, you will be locked into the lower rate until the CD matures.

Liquidity Risk

Some platforms offer high liquidity, allowing users to quickly enter or exit positions, but others may have lower liquidity, especially during market downturns. Additionally, transaction fees on blockchain networks (like Ethereum gas fees) can affect liquidity. Example: A sudden drop in cryptocurrency prices might lead to reduced liquidity on a platform like Uniswap, making it difficult to withdraw funds without incurring losses.

If you withdraw funds before the CD matures, you may incur penalties that reduce your overall return. This lack of liquidity is the trade-off for the security and fixed interest rate that CDs provide. Example: Withdrawing from a 3-year CD after just one year could result in a penalty equivalent to several months' worth of interest, reducing the effective return.

Regulatory Risk

DeFi platforms operate in a largely unregulated environment. This lack of oversight introduces significant legal risks, including the potential for fraud, loss of funds due to platform failure, and sudden regulatory crackdowns that could impact platform operations.

CDs are offered by banks and credit unions, which are highly regulated by financial authorities. In the United States, CDs are insured by the FDIC (Federal Deposit Insurance Corporation) up to $250,000 per depositor, providing strong legal protection for investors[109]. Example: If

---

[109]https://www.fdic.gov/resources/deposit-insurance/understanding-

a bank offering a CD fails, the FDIC ensures that your deposit is protected up to the insurance limit.

Complexity

DeFi Platforms:
Participating in DeFi platforms requires a good understanding of blockchain technology, cryptocurrency markets, and the specific DeFi protocols in use. Activities like yield farming and staking can be complex and require active management. Yield farming on a platform like Yearn Finance involves selecting the right strategies, understanding the risks of impermanent loss, and managing gas fees, making it more complex than traditional investments. CDs are straightforward and require little to no management. Investors choose a CD term and lock in a fixed interest rate. The principal and interest are paid out at the end of the term or rolled over into a new CD. Example: Investing in a 1-year CD is as simple as choosing the bank offering the best rate, depositing funds, and waiting for the term to end.

Security Risks

Cybersecurity Risks: DeFi platforms are targets for hackers due to the large amounts of funds they handle and the decentralized nature of the ecosystem. A security breach can lead to significant financial losses for users. CDs are among the safest investments available. They are insured by the FDIC in the United States, and the risk of losing the principal is virtually nonexistent if the CD is held to maturity. Even if the issuing bank fails, the FDIC will cover your deposit up to the insurance limit, ensuring that your investment is secure.

Return on Investment

While the returns can be high, DeFi platforms are often accompanied by substantial risks, including market volatility, smart contract risks, and impermanent loss. Providing liquidity on Uniswap might yield high returns due to trading fees and additional rewards in governance tokens, but these returns are subject to market conditions.

---

deposit-insurance?utm_source

CDs offer stable and predictable returns with fixed interest rates. The return on a CD is guaranteed as long as the investor holds the CD until maturity. However, the returns are typically lower than those offered by riskier investments.

Tax Considerations

The tax treatment of decentralized finance (DeFi) activities is intricate, particularly in jurisdictions where cryptocurrency transactions are taxable events. Participants may incur tax liabilities on both capital gains and income derived from various DeFi operations, such as yield farming and staking. For instance, in the United States, the Internal Revenue Service (IRS) considers earnings from staking and yield farming as ordinary income, taxable upon receipt. Subsequent transactions, like selling or exchanging these assets, can trigger capital gains taxes based on the appreciation or depreciation since acquisition[110].

Interest earned on CDs is typically taxed as ordinary income. The tax treatment is straightforward, and there are no capital gains considerations since the interest rate is fixed and there is no buying or selling of the CD itself. Example: If you earn $100 in interest from a CD, this amount would be added to your ordinary income and taxed according to your marginal tax rate.

Liquidity Considerations

DeFi investments can offer high liquidity, especially on well-established platforms. You can typically withdraw funds from a DeFi platform at any time, but high gas fees on Ethereum could reduce the net return.

CDs require locking up funds for a specific term, and early withdrawals often result in penalties. This makes CDs less liquid compared to DeFi investments, which can usually be accessed more quickly. Example: Withdrawing from a 5-year CD after 2 years might incur a penalty equivalent to several months' worth of interest, effectively reducing the return

---

[110]https://www.irs.gov/businesses/small-businesses-self-employed/digital-assets?utm_source

Table 19: DeFi platforms versus Certificates of Deposit (CDs)

Aspect	DeFi Platforms	CDs
Risks	High risk: Smart contract vulnerabilities, market volatility.	Low risk: Principal secured, interest rate risk. Example: Missing higher rates due to locked-in lower rates.
Market Risk	Highly volatile, tied to cryptocurrency markets. Example: Significant fluctuations impacting yield farming returns.	Low: Not subject to market volatility, fixed returns. Example: Stable interest despite market changes.
Liquidity Risk	Variable can be high or low depending on market conditions. Example: Reduced liquidity in downturns on Uniswap.	Lower liquidity, penalties for early withdrawal. Example: Penalties for withdrawing from a 3-year CD early.
Regulatory Risk	Largely unregulated, potential for sudden regulatory impacts. Example: Possible new regulations affecting operations.	Highly regulated, insured by FDIC up to $250,000. Example: Bank failures covered by FDIC insurance.
Complexity	High: Requires understanding of blockchain technology and active management. Example: Managing yield farming on Yearn Finance.	Low: Simple process, no active management required. Example: Investing in a 1-year CD at a fixed rate.
Security Risks	High: Targets for cyberattacks. Example: Poly Network hack resulted in significant losses.	Very low: Insured by FDIC, low cyber risk. Example: Security through bank insurance, no direct cyber threats.
Return on Investment	Very high potential returns, high variability. Example: High APYs and governance token rewards on Uniswap.	Stable and predictable, but lower returns. Example: Guaranteed interest rate on a 1-year CD.
Tax Considerations	Complex: Taxes on capital gains and DeFi income.	Straightforward: Interest taxed as ordinary income.
Liquidity Considerations	High on established platforms but affected by fees and market conditions.	Less liquid, with penalties for early access.

Popular Blockchains Used in DeFi

While Ethereum is the most widely used blockchain for DeFi, thanks to its robust smart contract functionality and large developer community, several other blockchains are gaining popularity due to their unique features and capabilities.

Ethereum

- Overview: Ethereum is the pioneering blockchain for smart contracts and DeFi. It supports a wide range of decentralized applications (dApps) and protocols, making it the backbone of the DeFi ecosystem.

- Strengths: Ethereum's large developer community, well-established ecosystem, and extensive tooling make it the go-to platform for DeFi projects. However, it has faced scalability challenges, leading to high transaction fees during periods of network congestion.

- https://ethereum.org

Binance Smart Chain (BSC)

- Overview: Binance Smart Chain is a blockchain developed by Binance, offering faster and cheaper transactions compared to Ethereum, with a similar environment for developing dApps.

- Strengths: BSC provides compatibility with the Ethereum Virtual Machine (EVM), allowing developers to easily port their Ethereum-based dApps to BSC. It has gained popularity due to its lower transaction fees and faster block times.

- https://www.binance.org/en/smartChain

Solana

- Overview: Solana is known for its high throughput and low-latency blockchain, capable of processing thousands of transactions per second (TPS) with minimal fees (median fee per transaction is $0.00064)

- Strengths: Solana's architecture allows for rapid transaction processing and scalability, making it an attractive option for DeFi applications that require high performance and low costs.

- https://solana.com

Polkadot

- Overview: Polkadot is a multi-chain platform designed to enable different blockchains to interoperate. It allows for the creation of specialized blockchains (parachains) that can communicate with each other and the main Polkadot relay chain.

- Strengths: Polkadot's interoperability and scalability make it a promising platform for DeFi projects that require cross-chain functionality and flexibility in choosing different consensus mechanisms or governance models.

- https://polkadot.network

Avalanche (AVAX)

- Overview: Avalanche is a high-performance blockchain platform that aims to provide a scalable and decentralized infrastructure for decentralized applications (dApps) and enterprise-grade solutions. It is designed to be highly customizable, allowing developers to create their own subnets with tailored rules and consensus mechanisms.

- Strengths: Avalanche boasts high throughput with low latency and near-instant transaction finality. It is also compatible with Ethereum, enabling developers to easily migrate or integrate their Ethereum dApps on Avalanche. Its consensus protocol is known for being highly scalable without sacrificing decentralization.

- DeFi Ecosystem: Avalanche has a growing DeFi ecosystem, including popular projects like Pangolin (a decentralized exchange "https://www.pangolin.exchange"), Benqi (a lending platform, "https://benqi.fi").

- https://www.avax.network

Terra (LUNA)

- Overview: Terra is a blockchain platform focused on creating stablecoins and stablecoin-based DeFi applications. It is known for its algorithmic stablecoins, such as UST (TerraUSD), which are pegged to various fiat currencies and stabilized by the LUNA token.

- Strengths: Terra's stablecoin system is designed to offer low volatility, making it ideal for DeFi applications that require price stability. Terra's ecosystem includes a variety of DeFi services, including payments, savings, and lending, with its stablecoins being widely adopted across multiple platforms.

- DeFi Ecosystem: Terra is home to prominent DeFi projects like Anchor Protocol (a savings protocol), Mirror Protocol (a synthetic asset platform), and the Terra stablecoins.

- https://terra.money

Fantom (FTM)

- Overview: Fantom is scalable, EVM-compatible blockchain platform that uses a Directed Acyclic Graph (DAG) architecture to achieve fast and secure transaction processing. It aims to provide a decentralized infrastructure for dApps, with a focus on speed and cost-efficiency (average transaction cost is 0.01$).

- Strengths: Fantom is known for its fast transaction speeds and low transaction fees, making it a popular choice for DeFi applications that require high throughput. Its consensus mechanism, "Lachesis", provides security and scalability without compromising on decentralization.

- DeFi Ecosystem: Fantom hosts a growing number of DeFi projects, including SpookySwap (a decentralized exchange), SpiritSwap (another DEX), and Scream (a lending platform).

- https://fantom.foundation

Cardano (ADA)

- Overview: Cardano is a blockchain platform that focuses on sustainability, scalability, and transparency. It is known for its research-driven development process and use of formal verification to ensure the security and robustness of its smart contracts.

- Strengths: Cardano's layered architecture allows for better scalability and flexibility. Its Proof-of-Stake (PoS) consensus algorithm, Ouroboros[111], is designed to be energy-efficient while maintaining security and decentralization.

- DeFi Ecosystem: Cardano's DeFi ecosystem is still in its early stages but is rapidly growing with the launch of smart contracts on the platform. Projects like "SundaeSwap" (a decentralized exchange) and MELD[112] (is a non-custodial DeFi protocol for web3 finance, providing cross-chain lending, borrowing and staking) are some of the notable developments in the Cardano DeFi space.

- https://cardano.org

Algorand (ALGO)

- Overview: Algorand is a blockchain platform designed to achieve high scalability, security, and decentralization. It uses a unique Pure Proof-of-Stake (PPoS) consensus mechanism that ensures quick and final transaction confirmation with low energy consumption.

---

[111] https://cardano.org/ouroboros/
[112] https://www.meld.com

- Strengths: Algorand's architecture allows for fast and secure transactions with low fees, making it well-suited for DeFi applications. It also supports the creation of smart contracts and decentralized applications that can be easily integrated into its ecosystem.

- DeFi Ecosystem: Algorand's DeFi ecosystem includes projects like Algofi[113] (a decentralized lending market), Tinyman (a decentralized exchange), and Yieldly[114] (a DeFi platform offering no-loss lotteries and staking).

- https://www.algorand.com

Tezos (XTZ)

- Overview: Tezos is a blockchain platform that focuses on self-amendment and on-chain governance. It enables users to propose and vote on protocol upgrades, ensuring that the platform can evolve without requiring hard forks.

- Strengths: Tezos's governance model allows for continuous innovation while maintaining network stability. It also features a highly efficient Proof-of-Stake (PoS) consensus mechanism, which is energy-efficient and provides strong security guarantees.

- DeFi Ecosystem: The Tezos DeFi ecosystem is expanding with projects like Plenty (a decentralized exchange), Kolibri (a stablecoin protocol), and Crunchy (a yield farming platform).

- https://tezos.com

Harmony (ONE)

- Overview: Harmony is a blockchain platform designed to achieve scalability without sacrificing decentralization. It uses a sharding-based architecture that allows for parallel transaction processing, which enhances throughput and reduces latency.

---

[113] https://algorandtechnologies.com/ecosystem/use-cases/algofi
[114] https://algorandtechnologies.com/ecosystem/use-cases/yieldly

- Strengths: Harmony offers fast and low-cost transactions, making it attractive for DeFi applications. Its Effective Proof-of-Stake (EPoS)[115] consensus mechanism is designed to prevent centralization while enabling large-scale participation.

- DeFi Ecosystem: Harmony has a growing DeFi ecosystem with projects like ViperSwap (a decentralized exchange), Tranquil Finance (a lending and borrowing platform), and DeFi Kingdoms (a gamified DeFi platform).

- https://www.harmony.one

Near Protocol (NEAR)

- Overview: NEAR Protocol is a blockchain designed to be developer-friendly and scalable, using a unique sharding technology called Nightshade[116] to achieve high throughput and low transaction costs.

- Strengths: NEAR's focus on ease of use and scalability makes it accessible to developers, allowing for rapid development and deployment of DeFi applications. Its sharding technology ensures that the network can scale without degrading performance.

- DeFi Ecosystem: The NEAR DeFi ecosystem includes projects like Ref Finance (a decentralized exchange), OIN Finance (a stablecoin issuance platform), and Aurora (an Ethereum-compatible scaling solution built on NEAR).

- https://near.org

MultiversX

- Overview: MultiversX (old name "Elrond") is designed for high-speed and low-cost transactions. It uses a Secure Proof-of-Stake (SPoS)[117] consensus mechanism combined with Adaptive

---

[115]https://docs.harmony.one/home/network/validators/definitions/effective-proof-of-stake-bidding-process
[116]https://defi-planet.com/2022/11/understanding-proximityfi-and-how-nears-nightshade-will-disrupt-defi/

State Sharding to achieve scalability. This platform launch of three new products (xFabric, xPortal, and xWorlds) aimed at supporting metaverse creators and users.

- Strengths: MultiverseX architecture allows it to process thousands of transactions per second with low fees, making it well-suited for DeFi applications that require speed and efficiency.

- DeFi ecosystem includes projects like Maiar Exchange (a decentralized exchange) and Utrust (a payment processing platform that integrates with DeFi).

- https://multiversx.com

Celo (CELO)

- Overview: Celo is a mobile-first blockchain platform focused on providing financial services to unbanked and underbanked populations around the world. It is optimized for mobile devices and aims to create an accessible financial system.

- Strengths: Celo's focus on mobile usability and its stablecoin ecosystem make it ideal for DeFi applications targeting global financial inclusion. Its Proof-of-Stake (PoS) consensus mechanism ensures that transactions are processed quickly and securely.

- DeFi Ecosystem: The Celo DeFi ecosystem includes projects like Ubeswap (a decentralized exchange), Moola (a lending platform), and Valora (a mobile wallet for accessing Celo's financial services).

- https://celo.org

Arbitrum

- Overview: Arbitrum is a Layer 2 scaling solution for Ethereum, (Layer 2 scaling solutions are protocols built atop Ethereum's

---

[117]https://coinmarketcap.com/academy/glossary/secure-proof-of-stake-spos

mainnet (Layer 1) to enhance transaction throughput and reduce fees by processing transactions off-chain while maintaining the security and decentralization of the mainnet), (A mainnet (short for "main network") is a fully operational blockchain where actual transactions occur and are recorded on a distributed ledger) designed to improve the speed and reduce the cost of transactions on the Ethereum network. It uses optimistic rollups to aggregate multiple transactions into a single batch, which is then recorded on the Ethereum mainnet.

- Strengths: Arbitrum offers lower transaction fees and faster confirmation times compared to Ethereum's Layer 1. It maintains compatibility with Ethereum, allowing developers to easily migrate their dApps to Arbitrum with minimal changes.

- DeFi Ecosystem: Arbitrum is home to various DeFi projects that leverage its scaling capabilities, including decentralized exchanges like Uniswap (Arbitrum version) and lending protocols like Aave, which have launched on Arbitrum to take advantage of its scalability.

- https://arbitrum.io

Optimism

- Overview: Optimism is another Layer 2 scaling solution for Ethereum, utilizing optimistic rollups to enhance the scalability of Ethereum-based applications. Like Arbitrum, Optimism bundles multiple transactions together and processes them off-chain, reducing congestion and fees on the Ethereum network.

- Strengths: Optimism provides faster and cheaper transactions while retaining the security of Ethereum's Layer 1. It supports all Ethereum-compatible smart contracts, making it easy for developers to deploy existing dApps on Optimism.

- DeFi Ecosystem: Optimism hosts several prominent DeFi applications, including decentralized exchanges like Synthetix and Uniswap, and lending platforms like Compound. These platforms benefit from Optimism's improved scalability and lower transaction costs.

- https://optimism.io

Arweave (AR)

- Overview: Arweave is a decentralized storage network designed to provide permanent, scalable data storage. Unlike traditional blockchains that store transaction data, Arweave focuses on storing large amounts of user data in a decentralized and immutable manner.

- Strengths: Arweave's "permaweb" enables users to store and retrieve data indefinitely, with a single, upfront payment covering the costs of storage forever. This makes it an ideal platform for DeFi projects that require secure, long-term data storage.

- DeFi Ecosystem: While Arweave is not a typical DeFi platform, it plays a crucial role in supporting the broader blockchain ecosystem by providing decentralized storage for DeFi applications and other dApps that need permanent, tamper-proof data storage.

- https://www.arweave.org

Internet Computer (ICP)

- Overview: Developed by the DFINITY Foundation, Internet Computer is a blockchain platform that aims to extend the functionality of the public internet, enabling it to host smart contracts, dApps, and DeFi protocols at web speed. It seeks to replace traditional IT infrastructure with decentralized alternatives.

- Strengths: Internet Computer offers high scalability, fast transaction finality, and low-cost computation. Its innovative consensus mechanism, Chain Key Technology, allows it to scale efficiently and support a wide range of applications.

- DeFi Ecosystem: Internet Computer is still in its early stages in the DeFi space, but it has the potential to support a variety of DeFi applications due to its high performance and scalability. Projects like Dfinance and Enso Finance are among the early adopters exploring DeFi on Internet Computer.

- https://dfinity.org

Ontology (ONT)

- Overview: Ontology is a high-performance blockchain platform that focuses on identity, data privacy, and decentralized trust frameworks. It aims to bridge the gap between blockchain and the real world by providing tools for building decentralized identity and data management solutions.

- Strengths: Ontology's focus on identity and data privacy makes it well-suited for DeFi applications that require robust user verification and data protection. Its multi-chain architecture allows for cross-chain interoperability and scalability.

- DeFi Ecosystem: Ontology supports DeFi projects like Wing Finance (a credit-based lending platform) and OIN Finance (a stablecoin issuance platform).

- https://ont.io

Flow (FLOW)

- Overview: Flow is a blockchain platform designed for the next generation of digital assets and dApps, with a particular focus on NFTs (non-fungible tokens) and gaming. It was created by Dapper Labs, the team behind "NBA Top Shot[118]".

- Strengths: Flow's architecture is optimized for high throughput and low latency, making it ideal for applications that require fast, scalable transactions, such as gaming and NFT marketplaces. Its resource-oriented programming model, Cadence[119], is designed for security and ease of use.

---

[118] https://nbatopshot.com

- DeFi Ecosystem: Flow's DeFi ecosystem is still developing but has the potential to integrate with gaming and NFT platforms, enabling new financial products and services that leverage digital collectibles and in-game assets. Projects like BloctoSwap[120] (a decentralized exchange) are exploring DeFi on Flow.

- https://flow.com

Kava (KAVA)

- Overview: Kava is a blockchain platform that offers a suite of DeFi services, including lending, borrowing, and stablecoins. Built on the Cosmos SDK, Kava is designed to provide secure and scalable decentralized financial applications.

- Strengths: Kava's cross-chain capabilities, enabled by its integration with the Cosmos network, allow it to support assets from multiple blockchains, including Bitcoin, Ethereum, and Binance Coin. This interoperability makes Kava a versatile platform for DeFi applications.

- DeFi Ecosystem: Kava's DeFi ecosystem includes platforms like Kava Lend (for lending and borrowing) and Hard Protocol (a decentralized money market). The platform also supports USDX, a stablecoin issued by Kava, which is used within its ecosystem.

- https://www.kava.io

ICON (ICX)

- Overview: ICON is a blockchain platform that aims to interconnect various blockchain networks through its decentralized network called ICON Republic. It focuses on interoperability and aims to enable seamless communication and transactions between different blockchains.

---

[119] https://cadence-lang.org/docs
[120] https://swap.blocto.app/#/

- Strengths: ICON's focus on interoperability allows it to act as a bridge between different blockchains, making it a suitable platform for DeFi projects that require cross-chain functionality. Its Delegated Proof-of-Stake (DPoS) consensus mechanism ensures scalability and quick transaction processing.

- DeFi Ecosystem: ICON supports several DeFi projects, including Balanced[121] (a decentralized exchange and lending platform) and Omm[122] (a money market and liquidity staking protocol). These projects leverage ICON's interoperability to offer cross-chain DeFi services.

- https://icon.foundation

Waves (WAVES)

- Overview: Waves is a blockchain platform that emphasizes simplicity and speed, allowing users to create and manage custom tokens. It provides a robust infrastructure for building decentralized applications (dApps), including DeFi protocols.

- Strengths: Waves' unique Ride[123] programming language is designed for ease of use, enabling developers to quickly deploy smart contracts and dApps. The platform also offers fast transaction speeds and low fees, making it well-suited for DeFi applications.

- DeFi Ecosystem: Waves has an active DeFi ecosystem, with projects like Waves Exchange (a decentralized exchange) and Neutrino[124] (an algorithmic stablecoin protocol) leading the way. Waves' native token, WAVES, is used for staking, governance, and transaction fees within the ecosystem.

- https://waves.tech

---

[121] https://balanced.network
[122] https://omm.finance
[123] https://docs.waves.tech/en/ride/getting-started#introduction
[124] https://neutrino.at

ThorChain (RUNE)
- Overview: ThorChain is a decentralized liquidity protocol that enables cross-chain trading of digital assets without the need for centralized exchanges. It allows users to swap assets across different blockchains in a trustless and decentralized manner.
- Strengths: ThorChain's unique architecture supports seamless cross-chain swaps, making it a valuable platform for DeFi projects that require interoperability between different blockchains. Its native token, RUNE, plays a crucial role in securing the network and facilitating swaps.
- DeFi Ecosystem: ThorChain's primary use case is enabling decentralized, cross-chain trading. The platform also supports liquidity pools, where users can provide liquidity in exchange for rewards. As a result, ThorChain is becoming an essential part of the cross-chain DeFi landscape.
- https://thorchain.org

EOS (EOS)
- Overview: EOS is a blockchain platform known for its high scalability, fast transaction speeds, and low latency. It is designed to support the development of decentralized applications (dApps) with a particular focus on usability and developer experience.
- Strengths: EOS's Delegated Proof-of-Stake (DPoS)[125] consensus mechanism allows it to process thousands of transactions per second with minimal fees, making it ideal for large-scale DeFi applications. The platform also provides extensive developer tools and resources.
- DeFi Ecosystem: EOS's DeFi ecosystem includes projects like EOSDT[126] (a decentralized stablecoin) and Vigor[127] (a

---

[125]https://www.ledger.com/academy/what-is-delegated-proof-of-stake-dpos
[126] https://github.com/equilibrium-eosdt/eosdt-js

decentralized finance network offering lending and borrowing services). These projects benefit from EOS's high throughput and low-cost transactions.

- https://eos.io

Zilliqa (ZIL)

- Overview: Zilliqa is a high-throughput blockchain platform that uses sharding to achieve scalability. It is designed to support decentralized applications (dApps) and smart contracts with a focus on providing high performance and low-cost transactions.

- Strengths: Zilliqa's sharding technology enables it to scale linearly as the network grows, making it capable of handling a large number of transactions. This scalability makes Zilliqa well-suited for DeFi applications that require fast and efficient processing.

- DeFi Ecosystem: Zilliqa's DeFi ecosystem includes projects like ZilSwap[128] (a decentralized exchange or swap platform) and Zillion[129] (a staking platform which estimated APY is %8.89). These projects leverage Zilliqa's scalability to offer fast and cost-effective DeFi services.

- https://www.zilliqa.com

Aptos (APT)

- Overview: Aptos is a high-performance blockchain platform designed for scalability and developer-friendliness. It leverages a move-to-earn model to incentivize developers to build on the platform.
- Strengths: Aptos' focus on scalability and developer incentives makes it a promising platform for DeFi applications. Its high

---

[127] https://vigordac.medium.com/vigor-protocol-redefine-defi-e91d41af5a61
[128] https://zilswap.io/swap
[129] https://stake.zilliqa.com

- throughput and low latency can handle a large number of transactions, ensuring efficient and responsive DeFi services.
- DeFi Ecosystem: While the Aptos DeFi ecosystem is still developing, there are promising projects emerging, such as Pontem Network[130] (a decentralized exchange) and Prime Protocol[131] (a Defi platform which you can deposit one crypto and barrow another crypto assets). These projects aim to leverage Aptos' scalability and developer-friendliness to offer innovative DeFi solutions.
- https://aptoslabs.com

Sui (SUI)

- Overview: Sui is a blockchain platform designed for performance and specific use cases, particularly NFTs and gaming network. It utilizes an object-oriented programming language and is optimized for low transaction fees.
- Strengths: Sui's focus on performance and specific use cases, such as NFTs and gaming, makes it a suitable platform for DeFi applications that require these features. Its low transaction fees and object-oriented programming language[132] (object-oriented paradigm, organizing software design around data, or objects, rather than functions and logic) can facilitate the development of complex DeFi protocols.
- DeFi Ecosystem: While the Sui DeFi ecosystem is still in its early stages, there are potential opportunities for DeFi projects to leverage its performance and focus on specific use cases. Projects that can capitalize on Sui's strengths, such as NFT-based DeFi or gaming-related DeFi, may find a niche within the ecosystem.
- https://sui.io

---

[130]https://pontem.network
[131]https://www.primeprotocol.xyz
[132]https://www.educative.io/blog/object-oriented-programming?utm_source

Injective (INJ)

- Overview: Injective is a blockchain platform specifically designed for derivatives markets. It utilizes zero-knowledge proofs to ensure privacy and security and offers cross-chain interoperability.
- Strengths: Injective's focus on derivatives markets and its utilization of zero-knowledge proofs make it a unique platform for DeFi applications. Its cross-chain interoperability allows for seamless integration with other blockchains, expanding its potential for DeFi.
- DeFi Ecosystem: Injective's DeFi ecosystem is centered around derivatives markets. Projects such as Injective Perpetuals[133] (a decentralized derivatives exchange) and Injective Options[134] (a decentralized options market) leverage the platform's features to offer a wide range of derivatives products.
- https://injective.com

Polygon zkEVM (MATIC)

- Overview: Polygon zkEVM is a layer-2 scaling solution for Ethereum that combines the Ethereum Virtual Machine (EVM) with zero-knowledge proofs. It aims to improve Ethereum's scalability and reduce transaction fees.
- Strengths: Polygon zkEVM's compatibility with the EVM ensures seamless integration with existing Ethereum-based DeFi applications. Its use of zero-knowledge proofs enhances privacy and security.
- DeFi Ecosystem: Polygon zkEVM's DeFi ecosystem is rapidly growing, leveraging its scalability and compatibility with Ethereum. Projects such as Aave V3[135] (a lending protocol), QuickSwap[136] (a decentralized exchange), and

---

[133] https://docs.trading.injective.network/learn/derivatives/perpetuals
[134] https://www.gemini.com/cryptopedia/injective-protocol-layer-2-decentralized-exchange-dex
[135] https://aave.com/docs/developers/aave-v3
[136] https://quickswap.exchange/#/

SushiSwap (an automated market maker) have migrated to Polygon zkEVM to benefit from its advantages.
- https://polygon.technology

Table 20: Selected DeFi platform's features, advantages, drawbacks

Platform	Key Features	Pros	Cons
Aave	Lending and borrowing protocol	Flexible lending terms, competitive rates	Complex interface, risk of liquidation
Compound	Money market protocol	Automated rate adjustments, supports multiple assets	Learning curve for new users, risk of liquidation
Yearn Finance	Yield optimization platform	Automates yield farming, offers various investment vaults	Strategies can be complex, risk of impermanent loss
MakerDAO	Collateralized debt position (CDP) platform	Flexible collateral loans, issues stablecoin (DAI)	Risky during market drops, liquidation possibility
Curve Finance	Stablecoin-focused exchange and liquidity provider	Low transaction fees, high yield opportunities	Limited to stablecoins, risk of impermanent loss
Uniswap	Decentralized exchange	Supports a broad asset spectrum, decentralized operation	Market volatility

Conclusion

In this investigation of DeFi, we explored the foundational blockchain technologies that empower DeFi ecosystems and discussed the various financial instruments and systems it innovates, from stablecoins to yield farming, and beyond. We identified the key components and roles within the DeFi space, such as liquidity pools, governance tokens, and the burgeoning field of machine learning-driven automated market makers.

Through a comprehensive examination of decentralized exchanges, lending and borrowing platforms, and the intricate workings of smart contracts, we revealed how DeFi not only mirrors but also extends traditional financial markets with enhanced flexibility, inclusivity, and transparency. We also addressed the risks inherent to these systems, including market volatility and technological vulnerabilities, underscoring the critical need for informed governance and robust security protocols.

As we look towards the future of DeFi, it is evident that the integration of these platforms into broader financial systems is inevitable. The increasing interoperability among blockchain protocols promises to further bridge gaps between isolated markets, enhancing the fluidity of capital and the diversity of financial products available to investors.

This book sought to illuminate the complex world of decentralized finance (DeFi). It aims to provide finance professionals, scholars, and enthusiasts with the knowledge and tools to understand and actively participate in this transformative field. As DeFi evolves, addressing its challenges and unlocking new opportunities, it carries the promise of reshaping the financial sector by making it more inclusive, efficient, and accessible on a global scale.

References

Alamsyah, A., Kusuma, G. N. W., & Ramadhani, D. P. (2024). A Review on Decentralized Finance Ecosystems. *Future Internet, 16*(3), 76. Link

Allen, H. (2024). The dark side of tokenisation. *Financial Times*. Link

Almeida, L. M., Muller, F. M., & Perlin, M. S. (2024). Risk Forecasting Comparisons in Decentralized Finance: An Approach in Constant Product Market Makers. *Computational Economics*. https://doi.org/10.1007/s10614-024-10585-6

Ammous, S. (2018). *The Bitcoin Standard: The Decentralized Alternative to Central Banking*. Wiley. Link

Ante, L. (2021). Smart contracts on the blockchain: A bibliometric analysis and review. *Telematics and Informatics, 57*, 101519. Link

Ante, L., Fiedler, I., Willruth, J., & Steinmetz, F. (2022). A systematic literature review of empirical research on stablecoins. *Blockchain Research Lab Working Paper Series, 28*, 1–22. Link

Antonopoulos, A. M. (2016). *The Internet of Money*. Merkle Bloom LLC. Link

Antonopoulos, A. M. (2017). *Mastering Bitcoin: Programming the Open Blockchain* (2nd ed.). O'Reilly Media. Link

Antonopoulos, A. M., & Wood, G. (2018). *Mastering Ethereum: Building Smart Contracts and DApps*. O'Reilly Media. Link

Aquilina, M., Frost, J., & Schrimpf, A. (2024). Decentralized finance (DeFi): A functional approach. *Journal of Financial Regulation, 10*(1), 1–27. Link

Auer, R., Frost, J., Gambacorta, L., Monnet, C., Rice, T., & Shin, H. S. (2021). Central bank digital currencies: Motives, economic implications, and the research frontier. *Annual Review of Economics, 13*, 697–721. Link

Auer, R., Haslhofer, B., Kitzler, S., Saggese, P., & Victor, F. (2023). *The Technology of Decentralized Finance (DeFi)*. Digital Finance, 6(1), 55-95. Link

Augustin, P., Chen-Zhang, R., & Shin, D. (2022). Reaching for yield in decentralized financial markets. *SSRN Electronic Journal*. Link

Aune, R. T., Krellenstein, A., O'Hara, M., & Slama, O. (2017). Footprints on a blockchain: Trading and information leakage in distributed ledgers. *Journal of Trading, 12*(3), 5-13. Link

Bashir, I. (2020). *Mastering Blockchain: A deep dive into distributed ledgers, consensus protocols, smart contracts, DApps, cryptocurrencies, Ethereum, and more*. Packt Publishing Ltd. Link

Beinke, M., Beinke, J. H., Anton, E., & Teuteberg, F. (2024). Breaking the chains of traditional finance: A taxonomy of decentralized finance business models. *Electronic Markets, 34*(1). https://doi.org/10.1007/s12525-024-00704-4

Bennett, D., Mekelburg, E., & Williams, T. H. (2023). BeFi meets DeFi: A behavioral finance approach to decentralized finance asset pricing. *Research In International Business And Finance*, 65. https://doi.org/10.1016/j.ribaf.2023.101939

Berg, C., Davidson, S., & Potts, J. (2019). *Understanding the blockchain economy: An introduction to institutional cryptoeconomics*. Edward Elgar Publishing. Link

Bhambhwani, S. M., & Huang, A. H. (2024). Auditing decentralized finance. *British Accounting Review*, 56(2). https://doi.org/10.1016/j.bar.2023.101270

Biais, B., Bisière, C., Bouvard, M., & Casamatta, C. (2019). The blockchain folk theorem. *The Review of Financial Studies*, 32(5), 1662-1715. Link

Birrer, T. K., Amstutz, D., & Wenger, P. (2023). *Decentralized Finance: From Core Concepts to DeFi Protocols for Financial Services*. Springer. Link

Blemus, S., & Guegan, D. (2019). Initial crypto-asset offerings (ICOs), tokenization and corporate governance. *SSRN Electronic Journal*. Link

Bodo, B., & de Filippi, P. (2024). Trust in context: The impact of regulation on blockchain and DeFi. *Regulation & Governance*. https://doi.org/10.1111/rego.12637

Bok, K. (2023). *Decentralizing Finance: How DeFi, Digital Assets, and Distributed Ledger Technology Are Transforming Finance*. Wiley. Link

Bourveau, T., Brendel, J., & Schoenfeld, J. (2024). Decentralized Finance (DeFi) assurance: early evidence. *Review Of Accounting Studies*. https://doi.org/10.1007/s11142-024-09834-8

Brekke, J. K. (2021). *Hacker-Engineers and Their Economies: The Political Economy of Decentralised Networks and 'Cryptoeconomics'*. New Political Economy, 26(1), 1-14. Link

Buterin, V. (2014). *A Next-Generation Smart Contract and Decentralized Application Platform*. Ethereum Whitepaper. Link

Caldarelli, G., & Ellul, J. (2021). The Blockchain Oracle Problem in Decentralized Finance-A Multivocal Approach. *Applied Sciences-Basel*, 11(16). https://doi.org/10.3390/app11167572

Capponi, A., & Jia, J. (2021). The adoption of blockchain-based decentralized exchanges. *Management Science*, 67(9), 5449-5465. Link

Capponi, A., Iyengar, G., & Sethuraman, J. (2023). *Decentralized Finance: Protocols, Risks, and Governance*. arXiv preprint arXiv:2312.01018. Link

Cartea, A., Drissit, F., & Monga, M. (2024). Decentralized Finance and Automated Market Making: Predictable Loss and Optimal Liquidity Provision. *Siam Journal On Financial Mathematics*, 15(3), 931–959. https://doi.org/10.1137/23M1602103

Casey, M. J., & Vigna, P. (2018). *The Truth Machine: The Blockchain and the Future of Everything*. St. Martin's Press. Link

Catalini, C., & Gans, J. S. (2016). Some simple economics of the blockchain. *NBER Working Paper No. 22952*. Link

Chaliasos, S., Charalambous, M. A., Zhou, L., Galanopoulou, R., Gervais, A., Mitropoulos, D., & Livshits, B. (2023). Smart contract and defi security: Insights from tool evaluations and practitioner surveys. *arXiv preprint arXiv:2304.02981*. Link

Champagne, P. (2014). *The Book of Satoshi: The Collected Writings of Bitcoin Creator Satoshi Nakamoto*. E53 Publishing LLC. Link

Chen, Y., & Bellavitis, C. (2020). Blockchain disruption and decentralized finance: The rise of decentralized business models. *Journal of Business Venturing Insights, 13*, e00151. Link

Chiu, J., & Koeppl, T. V. (2019). *Blockchain-Based Settlement for Asset Trading*. The Review of Financial Studies, 32(5), 1716-1753. Link

Chiu, J., Kahn, C. M., & Koeppl, T. V. (2022). Grasping decentralized finance through the lens of economic theory. *Canadian Journal Of Economics-Revue Canadienne D Economique, 55*(4), 1702–1728. https://doi.org/10.1111/caje.12627

Chohan, U. W. (2017). The decentralized autonomous organization and governance issues. *SSRN Electronic Journal*. Link

Cong, L. W., & He, Z. (2019). Blockchain disruption and smart contracts. *The Review of Financial Studies, 32*(5), 1754-1797. Link

Cousaert, S., Xu, J., & Matsui, T. (2021). SoK: Yield aggregators in DeFi. *arXiv preprint arXiv:2105.13891*. Link

Cumming, D., Drobetz, W., Momtaz, P. P., & Schermann, N. (2025). Financing decentralized digital platform growth: The role of crypto funds in blockchain-based startups. *Journal Of Business Venturing, 40*(1). https://doi.org/10.1016/j.jbusvent.2024.106450

Das, S., & Venkataraman, R. (2023). Incentivized third-party collateralization for stablecoins. *arXiv preprint arXiv:2309.11521*, 1–10. Link

De Blasis, R., Galati, L., Webb, A., & Webb, R. I. (2023). Intelligent design: stablecoins (in) stability and collateral during market turbulence. *Financial Innovation, 9*(1), 85. Link

De Filippi, P., & Wright, A. (2018). *Blockchain and the Law: The Rule of Code*. Harvard University Press. Link

Delgado Fernandez, J., Barbereau, T., & Papageorgiou, O. (2022). Agent-based model of initial token allocations: Evaluating wealth concentration in fair launches. *arXiv preprint arXiv:2208.10271*. Link

Demirel, E. (2023). Application of Blockchain-Based Smart Contract in Sustainable Tourism Finance. In *Blockchain for Tourism and Hospitality Industries* (pp. 122-138). Routledge. Link

Demirel, E., & Zeren, S. K. (2021). Developing smart contracts for financial payments as innovation. In *Research Anthology on Blockchain Technology in Business, Healthcare, Education, and Government* (pp. 1870-1889). IGI Global. Link

Demirel, E., Karagöz Zeren, S., & Hakan, K. (2022). Smart contracts in tourism industry: a model with blockchain integration for post pandemic economy. *Current Issues in Tourism, 25*(12), 1895-1909. https://doi.org/10.1080/13683500.2021.1960280

DiMatteo, L. A., Cannarsa, M., & Poncibò, C. (Eds.). (2019). *The Cambridge Handbook of Smart Contracts, Blockchain Technology and Digital Platforms*. Cambridge University Press. Link

Dotan, M., Yaish, A., Yin, H.-C., Tsytkin, E., & Zohar, A. (2023). The vulnerable nature of decentralized governance in DeFi. *arXiv preprint arXiv:2308.04267*. Link

Easley, D., O'Hara, M., & Basu, S. (2019). From mining to markets: The evolution of bitcoin transaction fees. *Journal of Financial Economics, 134*(1), 91-109. Link

Fan, S., Ma, X., Wang, W., & Chen, W. (2022). Towards understanding governance tokens in liquidity mining: A case study of Uniswap. *arXiv preprint arXiv:2205.12345*. Link

Friesendorf, C., & Blütener, A. (2023). Decentralized Finance (DeFi). Link

Frost, J., & Shin, H. S. (2020). Stablecoins: Risks, potential and regulation. *BIS Working Papers, 905*, 1–20. Link

Gans, J. S., & Halaburda, H. (2015). Some economics of private digital currency. *In Goldfarb, A., Greenstein, S. M., & Tucker, C. E. (Eds.), Economic Analysis of the Digital Economy* (pp. 257-276). University of Chicago Press. Link

Goghie, A.-S. (2024). Tokenization and the banking system: Redefining authority in the blockchain era. *Competition & Change*. https://doi.org/10.1177/10245294241258255

Gong, J., & Xu, W. (2020). *Cryptoeconomics: Igniting a New Era of Blockchain*. CRC Press. Link

Gorton, G. B., & Zhang, J. Y. (2021). Taming wildcat stablecoins. *SSRN Electronic Journal*, 1–45. Link

Gramlich, V., Guggenberger, T., Principato, M., Schellinger, B., & Urbach, N. (2023). A multivocal literature review of decentralized finance: Current knowledge and future research avenues. *Electronic Markets, 33*(11). Link

Gramlich, V., Guggenberger, T., Principato, M., Schellinger, B., & Urbach, N. (2023). A multivocal literature review of decentralized finance: Current knowledge and future research avenues. *Electronic Markets, 33*(1). https://doi.org/10.1007/s12525-023-00637-4

Grassi, L., Lanfranchi, D., Faes, A., & Renga, F. M. (2022). Do we still need financial intermediation? The case of decentralized finance - DeFi. *Qualitative Research In Accounting And Management, 19*(3), 323–347. https://doi.org/10.1108/QRAM-03-2021-0051

Gudgeon, L., Werner, S., Perez, D., & Knottenbelt, W. J. (2020). *DeFi Protocols for Loanable Funds: Interest Rates, Liquidity and Market Efficiency*. Proceedings of the 2nd ACM Conference on Advances in Financial Technologies, 92-112. Link

Hafner, M., Pereira, M. H., Dietl, H., & Beccuti, J. (2023). The four types of stablecoins: A comparative analysis. *arXiv preprint arXiv:2308.07041*, 1–25. Link

Hajek, B., Reijsbergen, D., Datta, A., & Keppo, J. (2024). Collateral portfolio optimization in crypto-backed stablecoins. *arXiv preprint arXiv:2405.08305*, 1–15. Link

Harvey, C. R., & Rabetti, D. (2024). International business and decentralized finance. *Journal of International Business Studies, 55*(3), 1–20. Link

Harvey, C. R., & Rabetti, D. (2024). International business and decentralized finance. *Journal Of International Business Studies*. https://doi.org/10.1057/s41267-024-00705-7

Harvey, C. R., Ramachandran, A., & Santoro, J. (2021). *DeFi and the Future of Finance 1st Edition*. Wiley. Link

Harvey, C. R., Ramachandran, A., & Santoro, J. (2021). DeFi and the future of finance. *The Journal of Financial Data Science, 3*(4), 8-35. Link

Homoliak, I., Perešíni, M., Holop, P., Handzuš, J., & Casino, F. (2023). CBDC-AquaSphere: Interoperable central bank digital currency built on trusted computing and blockchain. *arXiv preprint arXiv:2305.16893*. Link

Jensen, J. R., von Wachter, V., & Ross, O. (2021). An introduction to decentralized finance (defi). *Complex Systems Informatics and Modeling Quarterly*, (26), 46-54. Link

Jensen, J. R., von Wachter, V., & Ross, O. (2021). How decentralized is the governance of blockchain-based finance: Empirical evidence from four governance token distributions. *arXiv preprint arXiv:2102.10096*. Link

John, K., Kogan, L., & Saleh, F. (2023). Smart Contracts and Decentralized Finance. *Annual Review of Financial Economics, 15*, 523–542. https://doi.org/10.1146/annurev-financial-110921-022806

Karagoz Zeren, S., & Demirel, E. (2020). Blockchain based smart contract applications in tourism industry. *Digital business strategies in blockchain ecosystems: Transformational design and future of global business*, 601-615. Link

Kaur, S., Singh, S., Gupta, S., & Wats, S. (2023). Risk analysis in decentralized finance (DeFi): a fuzzy-AHP approach. *Risk Management-An International Journal, 25*(2). https://doi.org/10.1057/s41283-023-00118-0

Kirimhan, D. (2023). Importance of anti-money laundering regulations among prosumers for a cybersecure decentralized finance. *Journal Of Business Research, 157*. https://doi.org/10.1016/j.jbusres.2022.113558

Kitzler, S., Victor, F., Saggese, P., & Haslhofer, B. (2021). Disentangling decentralized finance (DeFi) compositions. *arXiv preprint arXiv:2111.11933*. Link

Kosse, A., Glowka, M., Mattei, I., & Rice, T. (2023). Will the real stablecoin please stand up? *BIS Papers, 141*, 1–20. Link

Krause, D. (2024). Assessing the risks of the Trump-backed WLFI governance tokens: A cautionary perspective. *SSRN Electronic Journal*. Link

Kwon, Y., Pongmala, K., Qin, K., Klages-Mundt, A., Jovanovic, P., Parlour, C., Gervais, A., & Song, D. (2023). What drives the (in)stability of a stablecoin? *arXiv preprint arXiv:2307.11754*, 1–20. Link

Langenohl, A. (2022). Making uncertainty operable: social coordination through game theory in decentralized finance. *Journal Of Cultural Economy*, *15*(5), 688–703. https://doi.org/10.1080/17530350.2022.2085146

Lehar, A., & Parlour, C. A. (2022). Systemic fragility in decentralized markets. *SSRN Electronic Journal*. Link

Lewis, A. (2018). *The Basics of Bitcoins and Blockchains: An Introduction to Cryptocurrencies and the Technology that Powers Them*. Mango. Link

Li, J., & Mann, W. (2018). Initial coin offering and platform building. *SSRN Electronic Journal*, 1-56. Link

Liang, K. (2023). Eden: An ultra-fast, provably secure, and fully decentralized blockchain interoperability protocol. *arXiv preprint arXiv:2311.17454*. Link

Liao, G. Y., & Caramichael, J. (2022). Stablecoins: Growth potential and impact on banking. Link

Lim, T. (2024). Predictive crypto-asset automated market maker architecture for decentralized finance using deep reinforcement learning. *Financial Innovation*, *10*(1). https://doi.org/10.1186/s40854-024-00660-0.

Lipton, A., & Treccani, M. (2021). *Blockchain and Distributed Ledgers: Mathematics, Technology, and Economics*. World Scientific Publishing Company. Link

Lloyd, T., O'Broin, D., & Harrigan, M. (2023). Emergent outcomes of the veToken model. *arXiv preprint arXiv:2311.17589*. Link

Makarov, I., & Schoar, A. (2022). Blockchain analysis of the Bitcoin market. *The Journal of Finance*, *77*(2), 803-847. Link

Meyer, E., Welpe, I. M., & Sandner, P. G. (2022). Decentralized finance—A systematic literature review and research directions. ECIS. Link

Mohan, V. (2022). Automated market makers and decentralized exchanges: a DeFi primer. *Financial Innovation*, *8*(1). https://doi.org/10.1186/s40854-021-00314-5

Momtaz, P. P. (2024). Decentralized finance (DeFi) markets for startups: search frictions, intermediation, and the efficiency of the ICO market. *Small Business Economics*. https://doi.org/10.1007/s11187-024-00886-3

Mougayar, W. (2016). *The Business Blockchain: Promise, Practice, and Application of the Next Internet Technology*. Wiley. Link

Nadler, M., & Schär, F. (2020). Decentralized finance, centralized ownership? An iterative mapping process to measure protocol token distribution. *arXiv preprint arXiv:2012.09306*. Link

Narayanan, A., Bonneau, J., Felten, E., Miller, A., & Goldfeder, S. (2016). *Bitcoin and Cryptocurrency Technologies: A Comprehensive Introduction*. Princeton University Press. Link

Nguyen, L. T. M., & Nguyen, P. T. (2024). Determinants of cryptocurrency and decentralized finance adoption - A configurational exploration. *Technological Forecasting And Social Change, 201*. https://doi.org/10.1016/j.techfore.2024.123244

Onder, I. Introduction: The Role of Technology in Transforming the Industry. In *Blockchain for Tourism and Hospitality Industries* (pp. 1-6). Routledge. Link

Outerlands Research. (2023). An evaluation framework for governance tokens. *Outerlands Research Blog*. Link

Ozili, P. K. (2022). Decentralized finance research and developments around the world. *Financial Innovation, 8*(1), 1–21. Link

Peters, G. W., & Panayi, E. (2016). *Understanding Modern Banking Ledgers through Blockchain Technologies: Future of Transaction Processing and Smart Contracts on the Internet of Money*. In *Banking Beyond Banks and Money* (pp. 239-278). Springer. Link

Pineiro-Chousa, J., Sevic, A., & Gonzalez-Lopez, I. (2023). Impact of social metrics in decentralized finance. *Journal Of Business Research, 158*. https://doi.org/10.1016/j.jbusres.2023.113673

Puschmann, T., & Huang-Sui, M. (2024). A taxonomy for decentralized finance. *International Review Of Financial Analysis, 92*. https://doi.org/10.1016/j.irfa.2024.103083

Qian, P., Cao, R., Liu, Z., Li, W., Li, M., Zhang, L., ... & He, Q. (2023). Empirical review of smart contract and defi security: vulnerability detection and automated repair. *arXiv preprint arXiv:2309.02391*. Link

Razzari, K., Lundström, M., & Wallvide, A. (2024). Decentralised Finance in the light of Institutional Theory. Link

Russo, C. (2020). *The Infinite Machine: How an Army of Crypto-hackers Is Building the Next Internet with Ethereum*. Harper Business. Link

Ryan, J. (2020). *Crypto Asset Investing in the Age of Autonomy*. Wiley. Link

Sadykhov, R., Goodell, G., De Montigny, D., Schoernig, M., & Treleaven, P. (2023). Decentralized token economy theory (DeTEcT): token pricing, stability and governance for token economies. *Frontiers in Blockchain, 6*, 1298330. Link

Saengchote, K. (2022). Decentralized lending and its users: Insights from Compound. *arXiv preprint arXiv:2212.05734*. Link

Schaer, F. (2021). Decentralized Finance: On Blockchain- and Smart Contract-Based Financial Markets. *Federal Reserve Bank of St Louis Review, 103*(2), 153–174. https://doi.org/10.20955/r.103.153-74

Schär, F. (2021). *Decentralized Finance: On Blockchain- and Smart Contract-Based Financial Markets. Federal Reserve Bank of St. Louis Review, 103*(2), 153-174. Link

Schär, F. (2021). Decentralized finance: On blockchain-and smart contract-based financial markets. *FRB of St. Louis Review*. Link

Schuler, K., Nadler, M., & Schar, F. (2023). Contagion and loss redistribution in crypto asset markets. *Economics Letters*, *231*. https://doi.org/10.1016/j.econlet.2023.111310

Schwiderowski, J., Pedersen, A. B., Jensen, J. K., & Beck, R. (2023). Value creation and capture in decentralized finance markets: Non-fungible tokens as a class of digital assets. *Electronic Markets*, *33*(1). https://doi.org/10.1007/s12525-023-00658-z

Seven, S., Yoldas, Y., Soran, A., Alkan, G. Y., Jung, J., Ustun, T. S., & Onen, A. (2022). Energy Trading on a Peer-to-Peer Basis between Virtual Power Plants Using Decentralized Finance Instruments. *Sustainability*, *14*(20). https://doi.org/10.3390/su142013286

Son, J., & Ryu, D. (2024). Competitive dynamics between decentralized and centralized finance lending markets. *International Review of Financial Analysis*, *96*. https://doi.org/10.1016/j.irfa.2024.103699

Sun, X., Stasinakis, C., & Sermpinis, G. (2024). Decentralization illusion in Decentralized Finance: Evidence from tokenized voting in MakerDAO polls. *Journal Of Financial Stability*, *73*. https://doi.org/10.1016/j.jfs.2024.101286

Sunyaev, A., Kannengießer, N., Beck, R., Treiblmaier, H., Lacity, M., Kranz, J., & Luckow, A. (2021). Token economy. *Business & Information Systems Engineering*, *63*(4), 457-478. Link

Swan, M. (2015). *Blockchain: Blueprint for a New Economy*. O'Reilly Media. Link

Tapscott, D., & Tapscott, A. (2016). *Blockchain Revolution: How the Technology Behind Bitcoin Is Changing Money, Business, and the World*. Portfolio. Link

The Wall Street Era is Over: The Investor's Guide to Cryptocurrency and DeFi, the Decentralized Finance Revolution. (2021). United States: DeFiYield. Link

Trozze, A., Kleinberg, B., & Davies, T. (2024). Detecting DeFi securities violations from token smart contract code. *Financial Innovation*, *10*(1). https://doi.org/10.1186/s40854-023-00572-5

Werner, S. M., Perez, D., & Gudgeon, L. (2021). SoK: Decentralized finance (DeFi). *Proceedings of the 3rd ACM Conference on Advances in Financial Technologies*, 220-235. Link

Xu, J., & Feng, Y. (2022). Reap the harvest on blockchain: A survey of yield farming protocols. *arXiv preprint arXiv:2210.04194*. Link

Zetzsche, D. A., Arner, D. W., & Buckley, R. P. (2020). *Decentralized Finance. Journal of Financial Regulation*, *6*(2), 172-203. Link

Zhang, R., Xue, R., & Liu, L. (2019). *Security and Privacy on Blockchain. ACM Computing Surveys*, *52*(3), 1-34. Link

www.ingramcontent.com/pod-product-compliance
Lightning Source LLC
Chambersburg PA
CBHW071527220526
45469CB00003B/666